Finance and Development

Westview Replica Editions

The concept of Westview Replica Editions is a response to the
continuing crisis in academic and informational publishing. Library
budgets for books have been severely curtailed. Ever larger portions
of general library budgets are being diverted from the purchase of
books and used for data banks, computers, micromedia, and other meth-
ods of information retrieval. Interlibrary loan structures further
reduce the edition sizes required to satisfy the needs of the scholarly
community. Economic pressures (particularly inflation and high interest rates) on the university presses and the few private scholarly
publishing companies have severely limited the capacity of the industry to properly serve the academic and research communities. As a
result, many manuscripts dealing with important subjects, often
representing the highest level of scholarship, are no longer economi-
cally viable publishing projects—or, if accepted for publication, are
typically subject to lead times ranging from one to three years.

Westview Replica Editions are our practical solution to the problem. We accept a manuscript in camera-ready form, typed according to
our specifications, and move it immediately into the production process.
As always, the selection criteria include the importance of the subject,
the work's contribution to scholarship, and its insight, originality
of thought, and excellence of exposition. The responsibility for edit-
ing and proofreading lies with the author or sponsoring institution.
We prepare chapter headings and display pages, file for copyright, and
obtain Library of Congress Cataloging in Publication Data. A detailed
manual contains simple instructions for preparing the final typescript,
and our editorial staff is always available to answer questions.

The end result is a book printed on acid-free paper and bound in
sturdy library-quality soft covers. We manufacture these books our-
selves using equipment that does not require a lengthy make-ready
process and that allows us to publish first editions of 300 to 600
copies and to reprint even smaller quantities as needed. Thus, we can
produce Replica Editions quickly and can keep even very specialized
books in print as long as there is a demand for them.

About the Book and Author

Finance and Development:
The Role of International Commercial Banks
in the Third World
Michael DaCosta

Although commercial banks have played an increasingly important role in providing capital to developing nations, many analysts argue that private financing poses risks both to borrowing nations and the stability of the international economic system. In response, Mr. DaCosta demonstrates that developing nations that adopt appropriate policies can gain substantially by drawing on private sources of capital. His analysis indicates that many criticisms of the role of commercial banks are unfounded and that debt problems in LDCs typically are related to inadequate reserve and external debt management policies in the borrowing countries themselves. Emphasizing that economic growth in LDCs often is constrained by balance-of-payment deficits, Mr. DaCosta shows that nations relying on private capital frequently experience higher-than-average growth rates and argues that the advantages of unconditional or untied aid generally outweigh the constraints imposed by the multilateral aid agencies. In conclusion, he outlines specific policies developing nations can adopt to reduce financial risk and, turning to the needs of the poorest of the LDCs, examines a variety of proposals aimed at increasing the flow of concessional assistance to those countries that cannot qualify for commercial bank funds.

Michael DaCosta is senior economist in the Research Department of the Bank of Guyana.

Finance and Development
The Role of International Commercial Banks in the Third World

Michael DaCosta

Westview Press / Boulder, Colorado

To My Parents, Irene and Philbert.

HG
195
.D32
1982

A Westview Replica Edition

Published in 1982 in the United States of America by
    Westview Press, Inc.
    5500 Central Avenue
    Boulder, Colorado 80301
    Frederick A. Praeger, President and Publisher

Library of Congress Cataloging in Publication Data
Finance and development
    (A Westview replica edition)
    Bibliography: p. 146
    1. Unerdeveloped areas--Finance. 2. Underdeveloped areas--Banks and
banking. 3. Underdeveloped areas--Financial institutions, International.
I. Title. II. Series.
HG195.D32 1982   332.1'53'091724   82-20276
ISBN 0-86531-917-0

Printed and bound in the United States of America

10 9 8 7 6 5 4 3 2 1

Contents

Tables

Acknowledgments

Many debts have been incurred in the production of this book. Perhaps the greatest is due to the Bank of Guyana for granting me study leave to pursue the research.

In its formation stages, Helen Agard and Deoranee Budhram were especially helpful in the search for data and other sources. As the work progressed, the librarians at the Bank, at The Institute of Bankers, London, and at UWIST provided valuable references.

Professor Glyn Davies, of the University of Wales (UWIST), deserves special thanks for many helpful comments and guidance throughout the research. Thanks are also due to Professor Gethyn Davies and Nigel Allington of UWIST for the useful discussions which I had with both on the issues arising out of the work.

The manuscript was patiently and meticulously typed by Cecelia France despite the presence of several barely-intelligible passages.

A final debt is due to my wife and parents for providing much encouragement and support throughout the research period.

Michael DaCosta
Georgetown, 1982

Abbreviations

BlS	Bank for International Settlements
DAC	Development Assistance Committee (of the OECD)
GATT	General Agreement on Tariffs and Trade
IBRD	International Bank for Reconstruction and Development - (The World Bank)
IDA	International Development Association
IDB	Inter-American Development Bank
IMF	International Monetary Fund
LDC	Less-Developed Country
LIBOR	London Inter-Bank Offered Rate
OECD	Organization for Economic Cooperation and Development
OPEC	Organization of Petroleum Exporting Countries
UNCTAD	United Nations Conference on Trade and Development
USAID	United States Agency for International Development

1
Introduction

The task of achieving rates of economic growth
sufficient to improve the standards of living of the
people of non-oil less-developed countries continues to
be of prime concern to policymakers both within and
outside the developing regions. This task is indeed
monumental. For example, recent estimates show that by
the year 2000, some six to seven hundred million people
could be living in absolute poverty.[1] To merely maintain the existing standards of living, a rate of growth
of at least 2.5 per cent, equivalent to the average rate
of population growth, would need to be achieved.

Growth requires resources of all kinds - human,
material and financial. Few developing countries have
had the internal capacity to generate sufficient levels
of financial resources to satisfy the requirements of
growth. As a group, therefore, they have had to supplement their domestic savings with large flows of external
grants and loans. In the years immediately following the
end of the Second World War and in the wake of the
apparent success of the Marshall Plan in Europe,
bilateral aid was widely regarded as the solution to the
resource gap faced by the developing nations. However,
after many years of experience with this type of
assistance, disappointment with the contribution of
official aid to growth is now widespread. As a result,

several plans have been advanced for increasing the
volume and quality of external flows to the less-
developed countries. Among these are:-
1. the SDR-aid link proposal,
2. the creation of a special institution
    to finance exploitation of minerals
    and other natural resources in LDCs, and
3. a guarantee scheme to facilitate access
    of developing countries to the inter-
    national capital markets.

While much work continues on attempting to effect
these and other proposals, multilateral and regional
financial institutions have, especially in the past two
years, adopted several measures aimed at raising the
level of assistance to LDCs. At the International Monetary Fund, the Compensatory Financing Facility, designed
to assist countries in meeting the balance of payments
consequences of export shortfalls due to external
factors, has been broadened to include shortfalls in
travel receipts and workers remittances. In addition,
the facility may now be used to compensate member
countries for increased costs of cereal imports. Also,
the Fund has moved into the area of medium to long-term
balance of payments financing with its agreement to
extend the repayment periods under its enlarged facilities to ten years. At the World Bank the introduction
of the Structural Adjustment programme, and emphasis on
the energy sector and on co-financing have been important
recent developments. Finally, regional development
banks have devoted much effort to mobilizing larger
flows of external finance for their respective areas.

In spite of these efforts and initiatives, it seems
clear that the official sector of the international
monetary system has failed to meet the growing financial
needs of the LDCs especially in the wake of the two

"oil crisis" periods of 1973-1974 and 1978-1979. Nevertheless it was over these periods that unprecedented rates of growth were recorded by developing countries largely as a result of balance of payments and development finance provided by international commercial banks.

A properly functioning international monetary system is one which ideally:

> ...provides a combination of international liquidity and adjustment mechanisms adequate to permit rectification of balance of payments disequilibria without imposing the necessity of severely deflationary policies on the deficit countries or obliging them to resort to balance of payments restrictions on current and capital account transactions, and over the long run provides a rate of increase of international liquidity adequate to support a steady growth of world production, trade and payments at levels as close to 'full-employment' of world resources as possible.[2]

While the I.M.F. has focussed primarily on adjustment mechanisms, the international commercial banks have shown themselves to be sufficiently innovative and flexible to enable the world financial system to overcome two major disturbances. This book stresses the role of the banks not only because of their critical importance during the oil crises and their aftermath, but also because it is felt that the contribution of international banks to economic development has been underestimated in both the literature on economic growth and by policy-makers in the LDCs.

Since the thirteenth and fourteenth centuries, banks and bankers have played a crucial role not only in the development of their own countries but also in that of foreign lands. Their importance in domestic financial intermediation has long been recognized in both theory and economic policy, but their potential for transferring resources internationally from surplus to deficit countries has until recently been largely ignored. That

banks should now perform on a global scale a task so well
done domestically, is not surprising given the degree of
interdependence in the world economy - in turn a result
of the ease and speed of international communications and
the growing internationalization of business.

It is argued here that LDCs will forgo higher levels
of growth, with all that it implies, for the welfare of
their people unless they make a concerted effort to tap
this large source of international savings. Traditional
sources of external finance have proven incapable of providing the volume of funds required by the developing
countries, and new proposals for larger flows seem
unlikely to be implemented in the near future. In such a
situation, these countries face the following options:-

1. to plead with donors for additional aid,
2. to try to expand their foreign exchange
   earnings from exports of goods and services, and
3. to seek additional sources of funds.

In a period of high inflation and generally tight fiscal
policies in the donor countries, option 1. seems to hold
little prospect for success in spite of much promising
and good intentions on the part of the donors. In the
long run, option 2. is clearly the most appropriate, but
export diversification to maximize foreign exchange earnings requires financing. By tapping world-wide savings
held in the international commercial banks and investing
them in viable, export-oriented schemes, the less
developed countries can aspire to a faster rate of economic growth, the benefits of which could improve the
welfare of hundreds of millions of people in the Third
World.

Chapter 2 presents an analysis of the relevance of
popular growth models to developing countries. It looks
particularly at those models in which savings and financial intermediation have a central role in promoting

economic growth. From this basis, a simple analytical
framework is developed showing how the international
financial intermediary role of banks can, by reducing
both the foreign exchange and the savings constraints,
increase the rate of growth of output and incomes in
LDCs. Chapter 3 reviews the historical role played by
banks in developing countries while Chapter 4, considers
the current need for savings in these countries emphasizing the serious need for external savings. Having
established this need, Chapter 5 proceeds to examine the
various non-bank sources of external funds available to
LDCs. These include bilateral and multilateral aid, the
international monetary institutions, and suppliers credits and other shorter-term sources of trade finance.
Since the international commercial banks are the major
supplier of external funds to the developing countries,
Chapter 6 is devoted to an examination of the banks as a
source of medium-term finance. Chapter 7, which is the
core of the book, examines the direct and indirect contribution of bank lending to the LDCs. It is concluded
that by virtue of the sheer volume of lending combined
with the many advantages of largely untied funds, this
contribution has been substantial.

An examination of the role of international banking
would not be complete without a mention of the many criticisms levelled against bank lending for balance of payments and development purposes. It is to this issue that
Chapter 8 turns. An important conclusion from the evalu-
ation is that many debt problems attributed to bank
lending per se are more accurately the result of inefficient domestic policies. Consequently, Chapter 9 examines the vital role of economic management in complementing the benefits to be derived from borrowing from the
banks.

In recognition of the special problems being faced

by the poorest of the less-developed countries, the pen-
ultimate chapter briefly depicts the problems and looks
at some proposals to increase the flow of concessional
assistance. These include the SDR-aid link proposal and
the guarantee scheme to facilitate LDC access to the
international capital markets. Chapter 11 incorporates
some thoughts on the present and future role of international banking in the provision of funds to the developing countries.

2
Theoretical Approaches to Growth and Development in Developing Countries

Theoretical concern with the issue of economic growth was expressed by the early classical economists such as Adam Smith, David Ricardo, and T.R. Malthus. For them, growth was a function of capital formation out of profits with the major limitation being diminishing returns to land and labour.

THE HARROD-DOMAR APPROACH

It was not until the period after the Great Depression of 1929-30, with its massive unemployment of labour, closed factories, and general stagnation of economic activity that the importance of growth resurfaced in the work of economists. The Keynesian Revolution had already shown that it was possible for the economy to stabilize at a less-than-full-employment position because of an inadequate level of aggregate demand. In the Keynesian, tradition, therefore, Harrod was concerned with determining the rate of growth required from one period to the next that would be sufficient to maintain the full-employment level. Unless such a rate of growth of national income was achieved, labour and the productive capacity of the economy would be unemployed or under-utilized. In seeking the more important factors on which growth depends, Harrod and Domar isolated two: firstly, the addition to output as a result of an increment in the capital stock - the incremental capital/output ratio, and secondly, the marginal propensity to save out of income.[1]

   Algebraically, where Y is national income, I is investment, K is capital, S is savings, the savings ratio, S = S/Y, and the capital/output ratio K is $\Delta K/\Delta Y$, the model proceeds as follows:

$$\Delta K = I$$
$$K = \frac{\Delta K}{\Delta Y} = \frac{I}{\Delta Y}$$

Now the Growth rate G = $\Delta Y/Y$

Since I = S

$$S = I/Y$$
$$K = I/\Delta Y$$
$$\therefore \Delta Y/Y = S/K$$
$$\therefore G = \frac{S}{K}$$

or the rate of growth of output equals the marginal propensity to save divided by the capital-output ratio. It could be increased either by raising the savings ratio or by increasing the efficiency of capital.

   In spite of the model's rather restrictive assumptions of savings as a stable proportion of income, fixed capital and labour-output ratios, the absence of technical progress or a foreign sector, the existence of a single, homogenous and well-behaved production function, and full-employment, it has been widely used by planners in developing countries. The usual procedure is to set a target rate of growth for the economy and to divide that figure by an estimated capital-output ratio, obtaining the required savings ratio. Fiscal measures are then implemented to extract part of the required savings from nationals, and foreign aid agencies and commercial sources are approached to provide the remainder.

   The attempt to apply fairly short-run Keynesian economics in general, and the Harrod-Domar model of growth in particular is not surprising since many LDC planners and policy-makers were trained overseas in the Harrod-Domar model and Keynesian economics, and in the absence of an alternative theoretical framework it was quite natural to apply this training on their return home. However, the limited relevance of a model designed for the short-run stabilization of a highly-industrialized economy like Britain to a poor agricultural or mineral-based country must also not be surprising. In reading the work of Harrod or Keynes one fails to see any serious considera- tion of the developing countries; it seems clear that it was not their intention that the models which they developed should be applied to these countries.[2]

It takes only a casual observation of all but the newly-industrializing LDCs to discover that the assump- tions of the Harrod-Domar model are far from appropriate, or as Reynolds states,

"...verge on a fantasy."[3]
The almost single-minded emphasis on physical capital in the post World War II period, and in the model is under- standable given the rapid recovery in Western Europe in the wake of large amounts of Marshall Aid. The success of the scheme led some economists, including the growing breed of "aid-experts" to advocate aid tied to physical capital as the most important factor in promoting growth in the developing countries. The consequent neglect of land, the agricultural sector, and labour has proved dis- astrous for the growth prospects of many countries which are only now trying to correct such mistakes.

From the point of view of financial policy, whereas the model treats savings as a stable proportion of income, research into the savings behaviour of LDCs reveals that much potential exists for increasing the average and mar- ginal propensities to save given the high degree of thrift practised by farmers and peasants, the yet under-developed nature of banking systems, unfamiliarity with financial assets as against physical assets, and the usually wide but unused scope for an active interest-rate policy to

attract potential savers. Finally, the model refers to a
closed economy when, in fact, trade and capital movements
are vital for growth in the developing countries.

In spite of the assumptions however, the Harrod-Domar
model is useful in highlighting two important elements in
the growth process of developing countries: the need for
savings, and for utilizing as efficiently as possible,
scarce capital resources. This remains its essential contribution to the theory of growth in developing countries.

THE NEO-CLASSICAL SCHOOL

The rigid assumptions of the Harrod-Domar model,
especially fixed capital and labour output ratios, led
neo-classical economists, one of the first of whom was
Solow, to investigate models containing flexible factor
proportions and factor prices.[4] The result was Solow's
use of the Cobb-Douglas production function:

$$Y = \partial K^\alpha L^\beta$$

where Y, K and L are output, the capital stock, and
labour, ∂ is a constant - indicating the state of technical progress, and α and β are exponents, showing the
elasticities of capital and labour with respect to output.
α and β sum to 1 - implying that a one per cent increase
in both capital and labour leads to a one per cent
increase in output.

Meade's extension of the neo-classical approach
results in a somewhat more sophisticated production
function:

$$Y = f(K,L,R,t)$$

where K, L and R are capital stock, labour, and land
respectively, and t represents technological change.
Where only land is fixed, growth can be expressed as:

$$\frac{\Delta Y}{Y} = \frac{aK \cdot \Delta K}{Y \quad K} + \frac{bL \cdot \Delta L}{Y \quad L} + \frac{\Delta Y^1}{Y}$$

where $\Delta K/K$, $\Delta L/L$ and $\Delta Y^1/Y$ represent rates of increase of
capital, labour, and technological progress, and aK/Y and
bL/Y are the elasticities of output with respect to

capital and labour.[5]

It is not surprising that like the Harrod-Domar model, the neo-classical growth model is not appropriate for the analysis of growth in developing countries. It was not intended to be. Rather it was developed to show that in the neo-classical world of full flexibility of prices and factor-output ratios, growth and full-employment could simultaneously be achieved. In any attempt to apply the model to LDCs therefore, several points need to be borne in mind. Perhaps the most important is that the fully price-flexible world is very distant from reality in LDCs where rigid structural differences, for example between urban and rural areas, may result in different wages and prices between sectors.[6] In more general terms, the whole basis of the classical system, resting, as it does, on the notion that full adjustment to equilibrium, i.e. full-employment, is achieved via the unhindered operation of the price system, seems ill-suited to less-developed economies which are far from being fully-monetized.

With respect to the Cobb-Douglas function itself, Mikesell[7] has noted that empirical studies showing the relationship between increases in labour and capital and the corresponding increase in output in the United States, show that the percentage increase in output is much larger than the initial percentage increase of either capital or labour. Finally, in common with the Harrod-Domar model, the assumption of land as fixed in its contribution to output which neglects the contribution of improved agricultural efficiency, and that of a closed economy, compound the degree of irrelevance of the model in analyzing the essential factors leading to growth in poor countries.

Many, much more complex and mathematical models of growth feature in the literature. However, their usefulness even in the industrialized countries has been

questioned by commentators and policy-makers. Hahn and
Matthews, at the end of their wide-ranging survey of the
literature noted:

> While not disparaging the insights that have
> been gained, we feel that in these areas the
> point of diminishing returns may have been
> reached. Nothing is easier than to ring the
> changes on more and more complicated models,
> without bringing in any really new ideas and
> without bringing the theory any nearer to
> casting light on the causes of the wealth of
> nations. The problems posed may well have
> intellectual fascination. But it is essen-
> tially a frivolous occupation to take a chain
> with links of very uneven strength and devote
> one's energies to strengthening and polishing
> the links that are already relatively strong.[8]

Mikesell in the course of his briefer survey of modern
economic growth models and theories is equally unenthusi-
astic. He states:

> There is a great variety of formal growth
> models, each of which employs a high level
> of abstraction. However, owing to the sim-
> plified assumption(s) and artificial nature
> of the problems considered, most of them are
> incapable of empirical testing and are of
> limited value either for explaining actual
> phenomena or for policy guidance.[9]

Finally, Sen, himself a noted expert on the economics of
growth, laments,

> It is partly a measure of the complexity of
> economic growth that the phenomenon of growth
> should remain, after three decades of inten-
> sive intellectual study such an enigma ...
> Part of the difficulty arises undoubtedly from
> the fact that the selection of topics for work
> in growth economics is guided much more by
> logical curiosity than by a taste for relevance.[10]

Not all interpretations of the growth process in
developing countries have been as complex as those
referred to by Hahn and Matthews, Mikesell, and Sen above,
and it is to these that the book now proceeds. The
LEWIS MODEL of economic growth was first enunciated by
A.W. Lewis in his celebrated article: "Economic Development with Unlimited Supplies of Labour."[11] He

characterized a typical developing country as being
divided into two sectors: the "subsistence" and the
"capitalist." It is important to stress that the subsistence sector is usually, but not necessarily, the same as
the agricultural sector and that the capitalist sector is
usually, but not necessarily, the same as the urban or
industrial sector. The urban workers existing at subsistence level were also regarded as a source of surplus
labour.[12] Surplus labour is attracted to the capitalist
sector by a wage rate that is higher than that obtaining
in the subsistence sector. Since the marginal productivity of labour is lower in this latter sector, migration
to the capitalist sector results in an increase in both
incomes and output, thus raising the rate of growth of the
entire economy. The process will continue until the
labour surplus is exhausted.

In a recent "revisit" to his dual-economy model,[13]
Lewis listed four channels through which growth in the
modern sector could be beneficial to the traditional. The
first of these is the employment of surplus labour which,
in addition to reducing population pressure where it
exists, provides higher wages and better opportunities
for migrating workers and their children, and enables cash
remittances to be sent back to the poorer areas.[14] Of
course, where the traditional sector suffers from neither
population pressure nor a stagnating economy, migration,
especially of its young, could damage the social and economic harmony of rural life.

The second channel is via infrastructural work
carried out by the modern sector such as the provision of
roads, railways, electricity, and water supply in so far
as these facilities improve productivity and the quality
of life in the traditional sector. In addition, by means
of relatively higher rates of taxation, the modern sector
contributes to the further development of the poorer
areas. The spread of knowledge, information and ideas is

also of potential benefit to the welfare of the people. This knowledge may be used to improve the efficiency of agriculture, enabling higher incomes and a better standard of living where it occurs. Finally, Lewis sees trade between the two sectors as mutually beneficial. The traditional sector ceases to organize its production only for subsistence purposes, and expands into production for the growing urban/modern sector. The availability of a wider market stimulates farming activity, provides employment for young farmers, and raises the level of income throughout the sector. The modern sector is provided with much-needed agricultural and farm products cheaply and reliably from within the country with which to sustain its workers.

Much of the criticism of the Lewis model centres around its assertion that the marginal productivity of labour is smaller in the traditional than in the modern sector, and is voiced primarily by those economists who regard the traditional or agricultural sector as more important to the process of growth in LDCs - at least in the early stages of their development. Schultz for example, states:

> There is no longer any room for doubt whether agriculture can be a powerful engine for growth... Once there are investment opportunities and incentives, farmers will turn sand into gold.[15)]

The evidence shows that in many LDCs, it is agricultural production and exports that provide the "engine of growth" for the economy. Indeed, the usual situation is for the traditional, agricultural sector to provide a surplus from which industrialization is financed - rather than vice-versa as Lewis implies. Further, the unfortunate experiences of many countries which tried to develop a modern, i.e. industrial, sector at the expense of agriculture but developed instead only severe balance of payments problems and enforced reductions in growth, are a common feature in the recent history of economic development of poor countries.

Lewis's response to these criticisms is that his traditional/modern dichotomy has been exaggerated and misinterpreted. He asserts:

> Nowadays a bogus history of economic thought
> floats around in which the economists of the
> fifties were rooting for industry to the
> neglect of agriculture, but this was not so.
> The economics of the 1950s was obsessed by
> balanced growth, arguing that development of
> industry alone would be constrained by the
> farmers' poverty, and that development of
> agriculture alone would turn the terms of
> trade against agriculture and bankrupt the
> farmers. As it happened most governments
> neglected agriculture for reasons of their
> own, but this was in spite of and not in
> accordance with economists' advice.[16]

In spite of the severe criticism of Lewis' main assumption, his dual-economy framework has become widely accepted as useful, for analyzing the problems of development in LDCs.[17] His "surplus-labour" concept remains relevant in much of the developing world as a consequence of high rates of population growth, the pressure on land, and heavy migration to urban areas by rural folk in search of a higher-paid job. More important, useful policy-measures suggest themselves from the analysis. Firstly, as suggested by Lewis, taxation may be used to redistribute incomes from the modern to the traditional sector and to finance essential infrastructure and other facilities in the latter. Measures to increase agricultural productivity and the incomes of the rural population may help to reduce the wage differential between town and country and therefore the incentive to migrate; they may also assist a country to be self-sufficient in food. Finally, in the field of international economic affairs, if the world is viewed as a closed economy, the dual-economy thesis is closely related to the "centre-periphery" view of relations between rich and poor countries shared by many ecomists in developing countries. However, in their view, no

benefits accrue to the poor countries on the periphery.
Instead, the rich, (modern) countries at the centre
attract skilled labour and cheap foods and raw materials
from the (traditional) periphery countries - thus perpetuating the latter's poverty. Much of the current discussion on "The New International Economic Order" centres
around attempts by the LDCs to correct this perceived
state of affairs.[18]

FINANCIAL INTERMEDIATION THEORIES

In spite of the wide differences in emphasis and
interpretation in the models mentioned above, a common
feature is present in all: i.e. they are concerned with
"real" (as against monetary and financial) variables such
as capital, labour and investment. While the marginal
propensity to save features in the Harrod-Domar model,
its importance and with it, the concept of financial
intermediation, is ignored by the assumption of a constant or stable marginal propensity to save out of
incomes.

Theories of the role of finance in promoting growth
in developing countries, though popularized by such economists as Shaw, McKinnon, and Galbis,[19] are not a com-
pletely new phenomenon. Perhaps the first modern economist to recognize its role was Joseph Schumpeter who
viewed the credit-creation function of banks as "...the
monetary complement of innovation"[20] - innovation and
entrepreneurship being central to his interpretation of
development. Already in 1955, John Gurley and Edward
Shaw had laid the foundations to the modern interpretation of the role of finance in their paper: "Financial
Aspects of Economic Development," in which they argued
that discussion of economic development in terms of
"real" variables only, results in

> "...an inadvertent undervaluation by eco-
> nomists of the role that finance plays in
> determining the pace and pattern of growth."[21]

More recent writings by Shaw, McKinnon, Patrick and
others, not only emphasize the importance of a strong and
efficient financial system in promoting growth, but also
point to South Korea and Taiwan as examples of empirical
support of their thesis. This can be summarized as
follows: The accumulation and efficient allocation of
savings are essential to economic growth. Financial
policy should therefore be deployed to maximize savings
in the financial system via an interest rate policy that
adequately rewards savers - yielding them a positive real
rate of interest. In order to efficiently allocate the
savings to competing uses, the criteria should be contribution to national income, and the relative real rate of
return on investment. The authorities encourage inefficiency by imposing ceilings on deposit and lending rates,
thereby diverting potential financial savings into "unpro-
ductive" uses such as real estate and precious metals.
An unfettered, efficiency-oriented financial intermediation process is therefore essential if growth is to be
achieved.[22]

Using South Korea as an example, McKinnon notes that
a rise in the official ceiling on nominal interest rates
from 15 to 30 per cent resulted in a net increase in the
real rate of return of about 11 percentage points on
demand deposits and 26 percentage points on long-term
deposits.[23] Further, the ratio of M_2 to GNP rose from 9
per cent in 1964 to 33 per cent in 1969 - reflecting an
increase in the level of financial savings available for
on-lending. Finally, in spite of the sharp increase in
interest rates, private borrowing from the banking system
remained buoyant. The rapid resurgence of the Japanese
and West German economies after the Second World War is
also partly attributed to the revival of their banking
systems.

Even more recently, in the Shaw/McKinnon tradition,
Galbis has attempted to show the effects of financial

intermediation on growth in a two-sector economy.[24] The
two sectors are the modern and the traditional: the former is characterized by high levels of technology, and
capital-efficiency, and a high rate of return on investment; the latter by capital inefficiency and low rates of
return on investment. The production functions of the two
sectors are:

$$Y_1 = F_1(K_1, L_1)$$
$$Y_2 = F_2(K_2, L_2)$$

F_1 and F_2 represent the two levels of technology with F_2
representing a higher level than F_1. K and L are capital
and labour respectively.

From Euler's theorem:

$$Y = Y_1 + Y_2 = r_1K_1 + w_1L_1 + r_2K_2 + w_2L_2, \text{ with}$$

r and w representing wage rates and rates of return so
that $r_2 > r_1$ and $w_2 > w_1$.

Since $K = K_1 + K_2$

an increase in K_2 at the expense of K_1 (leaving K constant) will increase Y as a result of the higher rate of
return to K_2.

Financial intermediation, by allocating credit to
more efficient sectors (or firms), can therefore lead to
an increase in Y.

The link between financial intermediation and growth,
therefore, is based on the fulfilment of two assumptions.
The first is that financial institutions are more efficient than others in the allocation of savings since by
virtue of specialization and economies of scale, (for
example, in terms of a country-wide branch network) they
have more information and a larger pool of skills at their
disposal. The second is that the credit-worthiness criteria of the banks should also satisfy the growth-orien-
tated needs of the developing economy. The accuracy of
this latter assumption is not as undisputed as it so often
appears in the literature on financial institutions.[25]

In assessing whether a borrower should obtain access to credit, some bankers in LDCs have tended to emphasize more often on security and ability to repay - in that order, rather than on the capacity for growth and the contribution to national output. As a result in many developing countries, savings tend to be allocated more to well-established government-owned or private busines-ses, many of which are involved in lucrative import/export and distribution activities of a basically non-productive nature, than to potentially very productive entrepreneurs who lack only finance and marketing skills. As Bhatia and Khatkhate note:

> The criterion of the credit institution in regard to loan management policies is only one of the many reasons for the absence of a link between financial intermediation and growth; others can be traced to the unwill-ingness of the institutions to provide tech-nical or management assistance to the local enterprises that are locked in unequal con-test with established industries because of a lack of marketing organization, project planning and experience. Very often the pro-duct has a good marketing potential, but the promoters are ill-equipped to organize it without technical assistance.[26]

The above comments are not intended to belittle the importance of banks, but rather to caution against the often unqualified assumption that financial intermedia-tion necessarily contributes to the growth of output in developing countries.

INTERNATIONAL FINANCIAL INTERMEDIATION

From the above, it will be noted that current theories of the role of finance in developing countries are concerned primarily with domestic financial interme-diation, i.e. the tapping of local savings for transfer into local investment. However, even a country like South Korea, cited by McKinnon as having developed a strong financial system, has had to supplement its domes-tic savings with external funds. Its external public

debt outstanding (including undisbursed) at the end of
1979 totalled $20 billion, of which $7.6 billion was owing
to financial institutions.[27] It is therefore regrettable
that the importance of international banks in channelling
savings from surplus countries or regions and on-lending
to deficit countries/regions bears little mention in the
literature on economic growth and development. One dis-
tinguished exception is Kindleberger who recognizes that
international financial intermediation via commercial
banks or capital markets can provide flows of vital international liquidity to LDCs faced with, for example, sudden
rises in the price of a crucial import or fluctuating
export receipts from the sale of primary products. He
writes:

> ...financial deepening, perfecting the capital
> market, and raising financial intermediation
> ratios, all have an international dimension
> that should be subject to economic analysis
> and made the object of policy formation ...The
> pendulum may have swung too far from the inter-
> national to the domestic.[28]

The other exception is Meier who, in the same vein as
Kindleberger, writes:

> ...The international saving-investment problem
> must be resolved, just as Keynes resolved the
> domestic savings-investment problem for domes-
> tic full-employment policies. Somehow, the
> savings of the rich countries must be trans-
> ferred into investment opportunities in poor
> countries. This requires a mechanism for inter-
> national financial intermediation and some
> source of deficit spending in the international
> system.[29]

and further:

> The fundamental point is that the international
> development problem is basically an investment-
> saving problem, but the international mechanism
> does not yet exist for its solution.[30]

It must be re-emphasized that these contributions to
the literature on the financial aspects of economic
development are so far the exception rather than the norm,
perhaps because the resurgence of large-scale bank lending

to LDCs is a fairly recent phenomenon beginning in the
early 1970s. Whenever international bank lending is mentioned, it is often in the rather limited context of the
so-called "re-cycling" of the OPEC surplus. Friedman, a
most experienced banker with much knowledge of developing
countries, notes that:

> What the banks have are deposits of which only
> a small part represents oil surpluses. On the
> other hand the banks have lending opportunities
> in LDCs which are caused by the high price of
> oil. Thus LDC deficits are not financed by the
> oil surpluses - they are financed by the credit
> extending capacity of the banks which greatly
> exceeds oil deposits.[31)]

It is clear, therefore, that whether or not an OPEC surplus exists, international banks, by their very structure
and orientation, will perform the very important role
within the international monetary arena of channelling
funds from surplus to deficit areas. This essentially
banking function is a natural extension of the bank's
earlier role in domestic financial intermediation. It is
also the result of the growing interdependence among
countries in all matters, and especially in the fields of
finance and trade. The intermediation function of the
banks seems destined to become even more vital as the
requirements of growth and development in the LDCs are
reflected in larger foreign exchange needs.

While the role of banks in promoting growth in
developing countries through international financial
intermediation is as yet largely unrecognized in the
literature, much has been written on the foreign-exchange
constraint on growth, usually from the point of view of
justifying aid flows to these countries. Three of the
theoretical works are mentioned here, those of McKinnon
(1964), Chenery and Strout (1966), and Michalopoulos
(1968). While they are somewhat dated, these writings
still form the basic theoretical argument for foreign
capital flows as a stimulus to LDC growth.

McKinnon's 1964 article[32] is primarily concerned
with the foreign-exchange constraint to growth. He argues
that since the foreign-exchange supplied may be used to
remove bottlenecks by providing vital goods required for
the growth process which cannot be produced locally, even
small amounts of foreign aid can have a favourable impact
on growth. If the resources provided by foreign aid are
used to enhance the foreign-exchange-earning activities of
the recipient country, its dependence on foreign aid can
be reduced progressively.

Similarly, Chenery and Strout[33] argue that foreign
aid may both supplement domestic resources and provide
goods and services essential to growth, such as machinery,
tools, and technical and managerial skills. Like
McKinnon, export growth is, in their view, the most
important means of reducing dependence on foreign aid and
embarking upon self-sustained growth.

Finally, Michalopoulos has developed a model showing
the growth-enhancing capacity of imports financed by
capital imports. Once his assumption that capital goods
necessary for investment cannot be produced domestically,
is accepted, (as it would be in most LDCs and even in
some industrial countries) the remaining arguments follow
logically; firstly,

> A foreign-exchange shortage can become an effec-
> tive barrier to a country's economic development
> by denying the country access to imported com-
> modities essential for its economic growth.[34]

and secondly, that, especially in the early stages of
diversification away from primary agricultural production,
foreign-exchange inflows can make a real contribution to
growth.

It seems, therefore, that the link between foreign
exchange flows and growth in developing countries has
already been established in the literature.[35] What is
now needed is that banks be incorporated in foreign

exchange constraint models, and that the foreign exchange needs of LDCs be linked to the financial intermediation performed by banks in the eurocurrency markets. However, as Machlup notes,

> There is a natural time-lag of economic analysis behind new economic developments, which explains the absence of scholarly investigations of money markets and capital markets in Eurocurrencies.[36]

In the absence of a comprehensive theory of international capital movements, a second-best alternative is an analytical framework in which the role of banks may be highlighted. The framework adopted here is the familiar two-gap model of development finance:

Begin with the usual national income identity:

$$Y = C + I + (X-M)$$

where Y = national income;

I = investment;

C = consumption;

X = exports of goods and services

and M = imports of goods and services

Now, let savings S = Y - C,

then, Y = Y - S + I + (X - M)

therefore M - X - I - S

or the foreign exchange gap equals the domestic savings gap.

The apparent simplicity of this conclusion, however, is misleading, for it implies that policies like those advocated by Shaw and McKinnon to close the savings gap will also reduce the need for external funds. Much care needs to be exercised in drawing conclusions from a tautology, and the conclusion of the two-gap model (M - X = I - S) follows from mathematics, not economic theory. The use of the model for policy purposes is misleading because, as noted above by the various writers and will be noted in Chapter 4, much investment, materials, and skills need to be imported, therefore,

domestic savings alone are insufficient to close the
resource gap at least in the short-to medium-term. The
advantage of bank lending in foreign exchange is that it
overcomes a most serious constraint to growth:- that of
foreign-exchange itself, at the same time as it supple-
ments domestic savings. In this context it is useful to
note Johnson who interprets balance-of-payments deficits
of LDCs in terms of an investment-savings relationship,
the proper analysis of which requires the use of a general
equilibrium approach which would integrate the domestic
and foreign aspects of development finance.[37)]

In the absence of a free international capital market
trading in all types of paper issued by developing
countries as was the case before the collapse of the market in the Great Depression of 1929-1930, the international banks will continue to be called upon to perform
the vital task of channelling savings to the poorer
countries of the world. As the following Chapter shows,
it is a task which they have carried out in the past to
great effect. In the 1980s, they are being called upon to
make a repeat performance.

3
The Historical Role of Financial Institutions in the Growth of Developing Nations

Commercial banks have contributed to the growth of many of today's more developed countries. These institutions, formed mostly by merchants or by the governments themselves, contributed by:

1. increasing the volume and availability of credit by issuing their own notes,
2. initiating, or at least participating in the financing of manufacturing projects such as textile manufacturing, and of public works such as canals and railways, and
3. less directly, by simply purchasing government bonds.

It may be useful and instructive, therefore, for developing countries now contemplating the possible role of banks, in helping to promote the development of their economies, to look more closely at the role of the early banks. The present Chapter is an attempt to present such a historical review.

As early as around the year 1200, bankers were progressing beyond the stage of mere money-changing and were entering into the field of banking as it is presently defined. In Genoa, for example, they began to accept deposits of both the current and the fixed-period type, to extend credit to merchants and traders, and were becoming

involved in foreign-trading and other business activities.'
Historical records reveal that they dealt in foreign currency and gave credit, to be repaid at the Fairs of Cham-
pagne in France, which at that time served as the great
foreign exchange dealing house of Europe.[1] The importance of the Fairs declined as the Italian banks moved to
establish branches in European cities such as London,
Paris, and Bruges, not only to finance trade between the
countries but also to lend to merchants and businessmen
of the countries into which they moved. It can be seen
that even at this early stage, bankers were helping to
facilitate the flow of trade between countries and were
beginning to lend overseas.

Towards the beginning of the fifteenth century, the
most important of the Italian banking houses was the
Medici Bank, founded in Florence in 1397.[2] Foreign
branches were soon established in Avignon, Bruges, Geneva
and London. In what were probably the precursors to
today's "country loans" by international banks, the Medici
lent heavily to monarchs, including Edward VI of England.
By the middle of the sixteenth century, government loans
were being syndicated (although that term was never used)
among groups of banks. Davis states that in 1555 such a
loan was floated successfully on behalf of the French
government. It was a ten-year loan consolidating previous
outstanding loans and at the same time provided some new
money at sixteen per cent.[3]

While extending their activities overseas by financing international trade and by lending to governments,
banks were at the same time contributing to the expansion
of commerce, manufacturing, and infrastructure within
their individual countries. In England, for example,
banks such as Lloyds were closely connected to local
industry. Sayers notes that the early banks "generally
originated as the ancillary business of traders, manufacturers, and mining concerns."[4]

Direct long-term loans to industry were common.
Often secured by mortgages on property or by simple pro-
missory notes, they were substantial by historical standards. Cameron quotes one example of a loan of £25,000 by
the London bankers Esdaile and Company, to Llanelly Copper
Company of South Wales.[5] The country banks also were
active in financing the Lancashire cotton and other cloth
manufacturing industry, the iron and heavy metal
industries, mining, and sugar refining - contributing to
both working capital and fixed capital investment. Also
noteworthy is the banks' contribution to the excellent
transportation system in Britain by means of investing a
proportion of their funds in canal and railway stock.

In Belgium, the banking system was perhaps even more
directly involved in industry.[6] Not satisfied with
merely financing companies, Belgian banks, notably Societe
Generale and the Banque de Belge,

> actively sought new firms, underwrote their
> stock issues, financed potential stockholders,
> held stock in their own names, placed their
> officers on the boards of directors of com-
> panies they promoted, and ministered to the
> companies' needs for both working capital and
> new capital for expansion.[7]

Among the leading Belgian firms of today are some which
were promoted and financed by these two major banks in the
period beginning around 1835. The firms promoted by
Societe Generale around that time included coal-mining
companies, ironworks, glassworks, a machinery and engi-
neering works, and the Antwerp Steamship Company. German
banks were also closely involved with industrial companies, not only by providing finance, but also by purchasing stock.[8] They continue to perform that function
today. In Russia, where the development of the vast Ural
region depended on improved transportation links, it was
the banks which assisted the State in financing railway
construction in the area.

Outside Europe, the "leading role" of the banking system in financing Japanese industrial growth has been propounded by Patrick[9] although Yamamura has disputed this thesis by pointing out that the banks only became interested in those concerns which were already well-established and viable.[10] In the United States, the rapid development of the West was helped by bank financing of canals, railroads and other public works.

Returning to the overseas operations of the large European banks, their lending to governments perhaps began in earnest in the early years of the nineteenth century. Between 1817, when the first foreign bond was issued by Barings of London on behalf of the government of France for 100 million Francs, until 1825, British merchant banks arranged several loans for European and Latin American governments. Nor were the big merchant banks the only institutions lending overseas. Many English country banks also participated in such activities. Between 1827 and 1833, Hentys of Worthing had invested some one-third of its funds in Brazilian, Danish, and Russian bonds. The Bucks and Oxon Bank's portfolio in 1869 included Russian, Turkish, Brazilian, Argentine, Peruvian, Portugese, and U.S. bonds, and the precursors of today's Lloyds Bank, Taylors and Lloyds of Birmingham, were, in 1821, investing in Prussian, Russian, and French stocks.[11] Such loans have continued to be granted, interspersed by crises of default, until the present time, and have resulted in the transfer of billions of dollars from Western Europe and the United States to developing countries.[12] To give some order of magnitudes, the total value of foreign investments from the major countries rose from under $4 billion in 1864 to $42 billion in 1913. During the same period, 4 per cent of Britain's gross national product and 40 per cent of her gross capital formation went overseas and by 1914 accounted for 47 per cent of total world long-term investment.[13]

Whether these large capital flows, a significant proportion of which was supplied or arranged by London and
New York banks, made a contribution to the development of
the recipient countries is, of course, an empirical question requiring a case by case study of each. Even when
such studies are conducted, it is very difficult to establish any direct causal link between external flows and
economic growth, given the complexity of the growth process. At the most, one may conclude that historically
there has been a strong association between external flows
of funds and economic growth in these countries facing a
foreign exchange constraint. Berrill, for example, mentions the role of foreign capital, obtained by the issue
of bonds in London, in the infrastructural development of
Australia and New Zealand. External funds were put to
similar use in Sweden and Russia; in the former, most of
the municipal debt was floated abroad and used mainly for
railway construction, while in the latter, one-half of the
national debt was foreign-owned by 1914. Norway used foreign capital extensively not only for railway construction, but also for the development of the pulp and paper
industry and hydro-electric schemes.[14] Hagen mentions
studies of Greece, Israel, and Taiwan which show some
association between large capital inflows and the rapid
post-war growth experienced by these countries. Con-
versely, declines in the rate of growth of Argentina,
Brazil, and Colombia in the early 1960s have been associ-
ated with reduced levels of foreign capital inflows.[15]
In addition, Horvat attributes the high rate of growth in
post-war Yugoslavia in part to the high level of capital
imports.[16] Further, Thomas quotes from a study of the
Canadian balance-of-payments done by Penelope Hartland
which shows that in the period 1900-1905, gross capital
inflows accounted for 26 per cent of Canadian gross domestic investment, while between 1906 and 1910, the contribution was 38 per cent.[17] Finally, Aldcroft concludes

his study of international lending between 1864 and 1913:

> without international lending on this vast scale,
> world economic progress would have been consider-
> ably less rapid.[18]

While certainly not underestimating the importance of
such factors as entrepreneurship, appropriate education
and training policies, proper management of the country's
human, material, and financial resources, and economic and
political stability, it seems clear that external funds,
either supplied or organized by commercial banks, played a
major role in accelerating growth in many of today's more
prosperous countries. The less-developed countries at
this stage of their development are in need of large flows
of external funds to cover the foreign exchange costs of
growth. International commercial banks have the capacity
to supply most of these resources. With the proviso that
the funds are utilized efficiently, this group of
countries stands to benefit in terms of enhanced growth
just as poorer countries benefited in the nineteenth and
early twentieth centuries to become today's prosperous
states. The following chapter attempts to establish the
current need for large flows of foreign exchange in
developing countries, after which in chapters 5 and 6, we
proceed to examine various sources of external funds, in
particular the international commercial banks.

4
The Current Need for External Financial Resources in Developing Countries

In chapter 2 an attempt was made at presenting the theoretical justification of the need for foreign exchange flows to developing countries. It was noted that the contribution of foreign financing to growth is usually expressed in terms of supplementing domestic savings and removing import bottlenecks. In this chapter, attention is turned to the current need for foreign exchange and to projected future needs. Before proceeding, however, it might not be inappropriate to re-emphasize the urgent necessity for growth in the group of countries under consideration.

In the more affluent societies it has for some time now, been fashionable to speak of the need for "limits to growth" and even of the undesirability of growth.[1] With relatively high levels of welfare benefits available and with the possible adverse social and environmental damage which may result from further unregulated growth, these warnings are perhaps justified. However, in the poor countries the desirability of growth is not a subject for debate. Poverty, as manifested by hunger, malnutrition, the inadequacy or even the absence of proper housing, high infant mortality rates, the shortage of such basic needs as potable water, and high rates of illiteracy, renders growth an absolute necessity. A leading expert of underdeveloped countries has written,

> The need for a higher growth rate in the [2]
> underdeveloped areas has become inescapable.

Beckerman points out that,

> A failure to maintain economic growth means
> continued poverty, deprivation, disease,
> squalor, degradation and slavery to soul-des-
> troying toil for countless millions of the
> world's population. [3]

Finally, with respect to Latin America, the President of
the IDB has said,

> Latin America has a pressing need to accele-
> rate substantially its economic growth, since
> on its achievement depends its social and
> political stability. This will have to be
> met by a major effort at increasing and
> improving the local savings and investments
> process, increasing exports..., holding down
> imports ... and finally, obtaining more exter-
> nal capital at an average lower cost. [4]

While the achievement of higher growth rates is not, by
itself, sufficient to alleviate the incidence of poverty,
a government's ability to attack the problem by means of
policies to assist the poor can be greatly enhanced if
based on a strong growth performance.

The objective of continued economic growth is important not only directly to the LDCs themselves, but also to
the industrialized countries. Slightly over one-quarter
of industrialized countries' exports are sold in developing countries. For Japan, the U.S.A. and the European
Community, the ratios are above average at 46 per cent,
36 per cent, and 38 per cent respectively. [5] In the case
of the U.S.A., its exports to the developing countries
are greater in value than those to the EEC, Eastern
Europe, the Soviet Union, and China combined. [6] The
importance of the LDC market to output, employment and
incomes in the industrialized countries should, therefore,
not be omitted from any discussion on the need for growth
in developing countries. [7]

Data on the recent growth performance of the group
published by the World Bank indicate that growth in gross

domestic product of all developing countries, excluding
OPEC capital-surplus countries, at constant prices,
declined from an average of about 5.9 per cent per annum
in the period 1960-70 to 5.1 per cent per annum in the
1970-80 period. On the same basis, growth in GDP per
capita fell from 3.5 per cent per annum to 2.7 per cent.
However, as the table below shows, the low-income oil-
importing countries, and especially those in Africa,
shared little of the prosperity enjoyed by the group of
developing countries. A major factor contributing to the
decline in growth rates was the recession in the industrialized countries during the 1970s which led to a slowdown in the volume growth of world trade and therefore in
LDC exports. With exports contributing between 20 and 40
per cent to GDP, the impact on growth was certain to be
negative.

The close link between exports and economic growth
only underlines the importance of foreign exchange in a
growing economy. Export earnings are vital because they
enable a country to acquire goods and services which are
not produced domestically. With the possible exception of
the newly-industrializing countries like Brazil, Korea,
and Taiwan, LDCs are heavily dependent on imported goods.
For the entire group of non-OPEC LDCs, imports as a percentage of GNP range from 25 to 35 per cent, and in some
countries like Honduras and Jamaica these ratios rise to
almost 40 per cent.[8] Since few countries earn sufficient
foreign exchange from exports to satisfy their import
requirements, external sources need to be tapped to supplement these earnings.

Prima facie evidence of the need for external borrowing lies in the persistence of balance-of-payments deficits on current account in non-oil LDCs, including those
which are regarded as being 'well-managed.' For example,
between 1973 and 1981, their payments deficits averaged
about $49 billion per annum; in the same period, net

inflows of external funds averaged $56 billion per annum, with the excess over the deficits supplementing international reserves.[9] These amounts are substantial and have augmented the foreign purchasing power of developing countries. External funds have helped to finance projects in agriculture, industry, infrastructure, social services, and have facilitated essential purchases of items as diversified as food, fertilizers, and heavy machinery. In the absence of these flows, the growth rates averaging 6 per cent per annum in the 1970s achieved by the non-oil LDCs would almost certainly not have been possible.

In recent years, however, in the wake of the world recession and constantly rising oil prices, the need for external financing has become much more acute. With respect to the oil situation, the price in early-1982 was almost three times as high as it was in 1978. As a result, the net oil-import bill of non-oil LDCs has surged from $18 billion in 1978 to approximately $36 billion in 1981, while the combined current account deficit is expected to climb rapidly from $39 billion in 1978 to almost $100 billion in 1982, or from 15 to 20 per cent of exports of goods and services.[10] This massive leakage of foreign exchange has had a severe negative impact on GDP growth rates in non-oil countries, and the era of 6 per cent growth per annum is almost certainly over in the absence of larger external flows in the short-to medium-term.

Combined with the oil price problem is the prevailing recession in many OECD countries where the rate of GDP growth has slowed considerably from an average of 4 per cent in the 1976-1979 period to an estimated 0.8 per cent in 1982. Lower activity levels and high unemployment rates serve to reduce demand for exports and to increase the need for borrowing on the part of LDCs. However, high interest rates in the United Kingdom and the United States,

have only added to the debt-service burdens of borrowing
countries in both nominal and real terms.[11]

The tables below show World Bank estimates of growth
rates and current account financing of non-oil LDCs up to
1980 and 1982 respectively.

TABLE 4.1

GROWTH OF GROSS DOMESTIC PRODUCT AND GROSS DOMESTIC
PRODUCT PER CAPITA, 1960-80

(Average Annual Percentage Growth Rates)

	GDP		GDP Per Capita	
	1960-70	1970-80	1960-70	1970-80
ALL DEVELOPING COUNTRIES	5.9	5.1	3.5	2.7
Oil Importers:				
Middle-income countries	6.2	5.6	3.9	3.1
Low-income countries	4.2	3.0	1.8	0.8
Asia	4.3	3.2	1.8	1.1
in				
Africa	4.0	2.4	1.7	-0.4
INDUSTRIALIZED COUNTRIES	4.9	3.3	4.1	2.5

SOURCE: World Bank: World Development Report 1981

Although in highly aggregated form, Table 1 highlights the
declining trend in growth rates in developing countries in
the 1970s. While the middle-income sub-group experienced
only a small downturn, it was the low-income countries, in
particular those in Africa, that suffered serious shortfalls. In per capita terms growth in incomes was negligible throughout the decade for low-income countries and
turned negative in Africa. World Bank projections up to
1990 show little improvement in these trends.

Table II below shows the foreign exchange requirements and sources of financing of non-oil LDCs between
1973 and 1982.

TABLE 4.2

NON-OIL DEVELOPING COUNTRIES: CURRENT ACCOUNT FINANCING, 1973-82

(In billions of U.S. dollars)

	1973	1974	1975	1976	1977	1978	1979	1980	1981	1982
Current Account Deficit[1]	11.6	37.0	46.5	32.0	28.3	39.2	58.9	86.2	99.0	97.0
Financing through transactions that do not affect net debt positions of which:	10.1	13.0	11.8	12.0	14.9	17.2	23.0	24.1	26.3	27.8
Net unrequited transfers received by Governments	5.4	6.9	7.1	7.4	8.3	8.2	10.9	12.3	12.9	13.6
Direct investment flows, net	4.3	5.3	5.3	4.7	5.3	6.9	9.2	10.0	13.6	14.1
Net borrowing and use of reserves of which	1.5	23.9	34.7	20.1	13.4	22.0	35.9	62.1	72.7	69.2
Reduction of reserve assets (accumulation -)	-9.7	-2.4	1.9	-13.8	-12.4	-15.8	-12.4	-4.9	-1.6	-4.0
Net external borrowing	11.2	23.3	32.9	31.2	25.8	37.8	48.4	67.1	74.3	73.2
Long-term borrowing	11.7	19.5	26.6	27.9	26.5	35.3	37.9	45.5	55.8	59.4
From official sources	5.4	9.3	11.4	10.8	12.6	14.2	15.4	20.5	20.2	22.3
From private sources	8.3	13.7	15.3	19.3	23.0	27.9	33.1	31.4	37.0	38.5
From financial institutions	7.1	12.6	13.8	17.0	19.4	23.9	32.4	30.1	35.5	37.0
Use of reserve-related credit facilities[2]	0.2	1.7	2.5	4.4	-0.1	0.5	-0.6	1.7	5.4	6.0
Other short-term borrowing, and errors and omissions	-0.6	5.2	3.7	1.0	-0.3	2.2	11.0	19.9	13.1	7.8

1) Net total of balances on goods, services, and private transfers.
2) Comprises use of Fund credit and short-term borrowing by monetary authorities from other monetary authorities.

SOURCE: IMF: World Economic Outlook 1982

It will be noted that from a fairly comfortable level of $39.2 billion in 1978, the current account deficit has climbed rapidly to reach almost $100 billion in 1981 with no sign of a reduction in 1982. Major factors in the deterioration have been the non-oil trade balance, (accounting for some 40 per cent of the decline), the oil trade balance (30 per cent), and net services, including interest payments on the external debt, (30 per cent).[12]

With respect to external borrowing, this is estimated to increase by $35.4 billion between 1978 and 1982. Of this, long-term official sources will have provided 23 per cent, the IMF and central banks, 16 per cent, other short-term sources, 16 per cent, and financial institutions, 37 per cent. It seems clear that the banks have responded remarkably well to the growing foreign exchange requirements of non-oil LDCs in a very difficult period. Even their critics concede that failure to meet these needs would have resulted in the world economy being in a much worse state than it is at present.

An important issue arising out of a consideration of the need for vast sums of external finance is whether increased mobilization of domestic savings could assist in reducing the volume of external borrowing. Domestic savings can do so in two ways. The first, and most obvious, is that in which the domestic currency is convertible into the currencies of trading partners. For example, since the Canadian dollar is convertible, Canadian savings may be used to acquire foreign goods and services. The potential problem here is that the external value of the Canadian dollar will fall if the flow overseas is in excess of external demand for the currency. The United States dollar suffered such a devaluation in 1973. Currency convertibility even in a limited form, is therefore useful to the extent that it reduces the need for large external borrowings.[13]

The second means through which increased mobilization of local savings may reduce the need for recourse to external finance is via investment in foreign exchange earning activities in both the merchandise and the service sectors, and it is to such a policy that most LDCs have been concentrating their energies and resources, having exhausted the possibilities for import-substitution. Contrary to the belief held in many quarters, savings to GDP ratios in many middle-and low-income countries appear quite healthy. In the low-income sub-group, India, Indonesia, China and Niger all had ratios between 19 and 30 per cent in 1979. In the middle-income group, El Salvador, Ivory Coast, Malaysia, the Philippines, Thailand, Tunisia, Yugoslavia and Zambia enjoyed similar ratios. The weighted average for the industrialized countries amounted to 22 per cent, the same as that of middle-income oil-importing countries, while that for low-income LDCs was 23 per cent.[14]

It thus appears that adequate domestic savings levels are not sufficient, at least in the medium-term, to alleviate the external debt problem. Foreign-exchange-earning and-saving projects are likely to take years to impact in the form of reduced external borrowing. In the meantime, the need for such financing will continue to grow and developing countries will need to tap all sources of external finance if present living standards are to be maintained and if some measure of growth is to be achieved. It is to an examination of these sources that the next two chapters now turn.

5
Sources of External Finance
to Developing Countries

In the heated debate over the large volume of external debt incurred by non-oil developing countries, it is sometimes forgotten that foreign exchange earnings from the export of goods and services finance about 70 to 80 per cent of all import requirements. In relative terms, therefore, external capital flows provide only a small proportion of the foreign exchange needs of this group of countries. Table 5.1 shows that in the 10-year period, 1973 to 1982, export earnings on average financed 75 per cent of total import requirements. Official external sources, i.e. bilateral and multilateral aid, financed about 8 per cent while private, including bank, financing accounted for 12 per cent.

TABLE 5.1

IMPORT FINANCING OF NON-OIL DEVELOPING COUNTRIES:1973-1982

(Percentage)

Merchandise Imports (f.o.b.)	96
Net Services and Private Transfers	4
TOTAL	100
	===
FINANCED BY:	
Merchandise Exports (f.o.b.)	75
Official Capital and Aid	8
Private Long-term Capital:	12
Direct Investment	(3)
Long-term Loans	(9)
Residual Flows	5
	100
	===

SOURCE: I.M.F.: World Economic Outlook - 1982

In what follows, an assessment of existing sources of external finance is attempted in the light of both their present and potential importance to the developing countries. Although the emphasis here is on financial flows, it is also acknowledged that non-financial assistance in the form of food aid and technical assistance, for example, may be of equal, or greater importance, especially to the least-developed countries.

1. EXPORTS

As Table 5.1 indicates, export earnings are the largest source of foreign-exchange to non-oil developing countries. In 1981, for example, such earnings provided some $327 billion out of a total foreign exchange requirement of $426 billion. Even for the least-developed net oil exporters, exports accounted for $21 billion of a total of $39 billion.[1]

Most LDCs are either primary-producing or mineral economies and this characteristic is reflected in the composition of their merchandise exports. In the low-income

sub-group, the share of primary agricultural commodities
in total exports of goods ranges between 70 and 99 per
cent for several countries.[2] In the middle-income sub-
group, while the concentration in primary commodities
remains high, mineral production provides a significant
portion of foreign exchange earnings in resource-rich
African and South American countries like the Congo,
Morocco, Zaire, Zambia and Bolivia, Guyana and Jamaica.
Some diversification into textiles and clothing has proved
important to many low-and middle-income countries like
Bangladesh, India, Pakistan, Egypt, South Korea, Taiwan,
Hong Kong and Portugal. However, progression into
machinery and other manufactured exports has been achieved
by only a few of the higher-income countries.[3] It is
perhaps not surprising, therefore, to find that it is
these countries which have achieved above average real
rates of growth.[4]

Approximately 70 per cent of merchandise exports
from developing countries are purchased by the industrial
countries with the remainder sold within the LDC group.
As a result of this heavy dependence, the economies of
LDCs are particularly vulnerable to the behaviour of
demand in the developed countries. In periods of sluggish
demand, LDC exports are often among the first to suffer;
for example, between 1974 and 1975, exports from non-oil
developing countries fell from $97.8 billion to $93.9
billion.[5] Of course, one may argue that the corollary to
all this is that the industrial countries are similarly
dependent on the LDCs for the bulk of their raw materials.
While this might indeed be the case, no commodity cartel,
except OPEC, has managed to benefit from a monopoly position in spite of the rapid increase in the number of producers' association[6] and more intense consideration of
new pricing strategies by existing associations - influenced by the OPEC action.[7]

In addition to their marked vulnerability to economic
fluctuations in the developed countries, export earnings
of LDCs suffer from an additional destabilizing influence
in the form of widely fluctuating export prices. IMF data
indicate that market prices of primary products (except
petroleum) exported by developing countries, increased by
28 per cent in 1974, but declined by 18 per cent in 1975:
a cumulative movement of 46 per cent in two years! These
may have been extraordinary years, but again in 1977,
these prices increased by about 20 per cent, only to fall
by 5 per cent in the following year.[8]

Such fluctuations render economic management and
stable growth very elusive and tax to the limit the capa-
bilities of policymakers. The inability to manage the
effects of wide variations in export earnings through
external borrowing, reserve management, and offsetting
demand management policies, has been a major reason for so
much instability demonstrated by the economies of the
developing countries. To the extent that some countries
have managed to diversify into manufactured exports, the
degree of instability has been reduced. However, the
success of the LDCs in their efforts to diversify exports
should not be overestimated. The GATT's preliminary
assessment of trade developments in 1981 indicates that
there was no volume growth of world trade and that in
dollar terms there was a decline of 1 per cent. World
exports of manufactures in volume terms expanded by only
3 per cent.[9] IMF data for 1981 show that in both volume
and value terms, major LDC exporters of manufactures
faced the lowest percentage increases since 1975.[10]

In attempting to escape the foreign exchange instability caused by price fluctuations of primary products,
however, developing countries face a potentially more
damaging obstacle: that of protectionism against manufactured exports of LDCs in developed-country markets.[11]

Motivated by the desire to prolong the life of industries
which have lost their comparative advantage to similar
industries in the developing countries, lobbies of both
employers and trade unions concerned have, since the
early nineteen-sixties, been partly successful in persua-
ding governments to impose restrictions on the exports of
developing countries. The exports most affected by protectionism are textiles and clothing, footwear, electric
consumer durables, and steel. The hardest-hit countries
are those which have proved very cost-efficient in the
production of such goods, for example, Hong Kong, Korea,
Taiwan, and to a less extent, in the field of textiles,
Bangladesh, India, and Pakistan. Quantitative estimates
of the foreign exchange earnings lost as a result of this
policy are difficult to find, but they tend to start
around $10 to $20 billion per year.[12]

In both prosperous and lean times, governments of
developed countries have been persuaded to implement more
and more stringent protectionist policies. An example is
the so-called "voluntary" controls by LDCs on their
exports which are, in fact, nothing more than disguised
export quotas imposed by industrialized trading partners.
However, at the same time, and with the substantial
assistance of official export credit agencies, the
latter's exporters are urged to maximize sales to developing countries. Ohlin notes that such agencies

> ... encourage unscrupulous salesmanship which
> takes advantage of the lack of experience or
> the understaffing of government agencies in
> developing countries.[13]

Prospects for a fall in the degree of protectionism
in the immediate future are not promising. The outcome
of the recent round of Multilateral Trade Negotiations
(MTN) provides for only some reduction in tariffs on LDC
exports with nothing being conceded by the developed
nations with respect to quantitative restrictions. In
any case, given the current recession in OECD countries,

pressures for increased protection are mounting and it
will be extremely difficult for legislatures to put into
effect even the tariff reductions agreed at the MTN.

As the most important source of external finance in
developing countries, exports face a serious threat from
the mood of protectionism now so prevalent in the industrial countries. If the governments of these latter
countries have a sincere interest in the welfare of the
people of the poorer regions, a reduction in the level of
protectionism should comprise the major policy measure to
be implemented.

For LDCs seeking adequate rates of growth and
improved access to banking and capital markets there is
little alternative in the long run but to continue, in
spite of the barriers, to maximize exports while attempting to diversify into those areas dictated by their
resource endowments and capability, without simultaneously
placing pressures on the balance of payments.

2. OFFICIAL AID

Table 5.1 shows that official sources of capital and
aid financed 8 per cent of the imports of non-oil
developing countries in the decade ending 1982. These
official sources comprise bilateral aid from OECD, OPEC,
and the Centrally-Planned countries together with assistance from the multilateral institutions such as the IBRD
and IMF, the European Development Fund, and OPEC institutions like the Arab Fund for Social and Economic
Development and the Islamic Development Bank. In this
section, the emphasis is placed on bilateral aid from the
industrialized, and oil-surplus economies.

OECD

The data in Table 5.2 show that in the ten years to
1980, net disbursements of bilateral assistance from OECD
countries rose from $6.6 billion to $19.9 billion. At
constant 1979 prices, however, the increase is less significant, moving from about $15.5 billion in 1971 to $18.3

billion in 1980. In the same period, total net concessional aid disbursements, including those to multilateral
agencies, advanced from about $8 billion to $26.8 billion
in nominal, and from $18.2 billion to $24.5 billion in
constant 1979 dollars. In terms of GNP, however, the percentage of development assistance from the industrial
countries has been virtually stagnant since the late
1960s at around 0.4 per cent. This stagnation is, to a
large extent, attributable to the aid-giving behaviour of
the most affluent of the industrialized countries.
Expressed as a percentage of GNP, net development assistance[14] to the LDCs and multilateral agencies in the
period 1970-1980 fell from 0.32 to 0.27 per cent in the
United States.[15] Indeed, excluding the U.S., the
ODA/GNP ratio was 0.43 per cent in 1980. It has been the
smaller countries like the Netherlands, and the Scanda-
navian countries which have managed to devote increasing
proportions of their GNP to assisting the poor countries.

The stagnation of aid/GNP ratios should not conceal
the fact that in real terms, concessional aid has
increased on average by 3½ per cent per annum between 1971
and 1980. In 1980, the real increase was 9 per cent.
This is in keeping with stated OECD policy that:

> ... international transfers, including aid on
> the right terms and in support of broad-based
> development, are indispensable if the poorer
> countries are to achieve accelerated develop-
> ment and there is to be a chance of eradica-
> ting absolute human poverty in the foreseeable
> future.[16]

Nevertheless, some caution concerning the maintenance of
the real rate of growth of OECD concessional aid would
seem to be in order in the light of historical trends and
current attitudes in some major donor countries. At a
meeting of the Development Assistance Committee of OECD in
1979, it was indicated that official aid from the group
would "... probably increase" in real terms in 1980, that
U.S. aid disbursements would "almost certainly" increase,

that the U.K. "had promised" to maintain the real value
of its contribution, and that Japan and West Germany were
"stepping-up" their aid budgets.[17] At about the same
time, however, the Chancellor the British Exchequer was
quoted as saying,

> The ability of the industrialized countries
> to help the poorer countries has, at least
> for the time being, diminished.[18]

Later, it was reported that the increase in foreign economic aid requested by the President of the United States
for fiscal year 1980/81 amounted to some $200 million -
which was a fall in real terms.[19]

TABLE 5.2

TOTAL NET RESOURCE RECEIPTS OF DEVELOPING COUNTRIES FROM ALL SOURCES

Net Disbursements in US$ Billion

	1971	1973	1974	1975	1976	1977	1978	1979	1980
Official Development Assistance	9.29	11.62	15.33	19.33	19.02	20.16	23.75	28.91	33.46
I. Bilateral									
(a) DAC Countries	6.33	7.09	8.23	9.81	9.50	10.08	13.12	15.91	17.64
(b) OPEC Countries	0.37	1.22	3.02	4.92	4.54	3.94	3.25	4.93	6.11
(c) CMEA Countries	1.26	1.35	1.26	0.73	1.05	1.09	1.28	1.75	1.80
(d) Other Countries	..	..	..	0.03	0.06	0.08	0.10	0.12	0.20
II. Multilateral Agencies	1.33	1.96	2.82	3.84	3.87	4.97	6.00	6.20	(7.71)
of which OPEC Financed	-	-	0.12	0.16	0.42	1.23	0.96	0.26	0.26
Non-concessional Flows	11.80	19.75	19.71	34.34	38.57	43.39	56.08	54.95	55.49
I. Bilateral									
(a) Direct Investment	3.31	4.72	1.89	11.51	8.64	9.59	11.83	13.62	13.69
(b) Bank Sector	3.30	9.70	10.00	12.00	15.00	13.20	22.67	19.67	} 18.00
(c) Bond Lending	0.58	0.58	2.40	0.42	1.22	1.11	1.22	1.14	
(d) Private Export Credits	2.71	1.15	0.86	4.42	7.22	9.11	10.22	9.49	12.20
(e) Official Export Credits	0.71	1.18	0.65	1.22	1.39	1.48	2.15	1.72	2.46
(f) DAC Other Official	0.28	0.90	0.92	0.56	0.57	0.48	0.89	0.95	2.24
(g) OPEC Countries	0.19	0.14	0.09	1.50	1.61	0.89	(1.01)	(1.00)	} (1.00)
(h) CMEA Countries	0.10	0.10	0.09	0.09	0.12	0.11	0.10	(1.00)	
II. Multilateral	0.90	1.28	1.83	2.58	2.68	2.94	3.09	4.16	(4.80)
of which: OPEC Financed	-	-	0.02	0.06	0.13	0.27	0.16	0.22	0.14
Total Receipts	21.09	31.37	35.04	53.67	57.59	63.35	79.83	(83.86)	(88.95)
Memorandum Items:									
Private Sector Grants	0.91	1.37	1.22	1.34	1.35	1.49	1.65	1.95	2.31
IMF Purchases Net	0.05	0.36	1.74	3.24	2.98	-0.43	-0.93	-	2.61
IMF Trust Fund (incl. under ODA II above)	-	-	-	-	-	0.18	0.86	0.68	1.64

(a) Excluding (i) bond lending and (ii) export credits extended by banks which are included under private export credits. Includes loans by branches of OECD banks located in off-shore centres, and for 1980 participation of non-OECD banks in international syndicates.

(b) Drawings minus repayments including reserve tranches (amounting to $103 million in 1979 and $309 million in 1980) but excluding loans by the IMF Trust Fund included under multilateral ODA above. SOURCE: OECD: "Development Corporation - 1981 Review." OECD-Paris-1981.

A lack of total commitment on the part of all industrial countries combined with increasing budgetary and balance of payments constraints appear to be the main factors underlying the present trends in aid-giving.[20] But for some time now there has been reason for much scepticism concerning both the professed motive of concern for the poor and the seriousness of the constraints to aid-giving so often expressed by aid donors. McBean and Balasubramanyam recall John Kennedy's statement to the Senate Committee on Foreign Relations,

> Foreign aid is a method by which the United States maintains a position of influence and control around the world, and sustains a good many countries which would definitely collapse, or pass into the Communist bloc. [21]

Mr. Neil Marten, Minister for Overseas Development in the British Foreign Office stated that aid from the Overseas Development Administration would now be directed to more countries which might be of benefit to the U.K. in terms of trade, strategic, or political purposes.[22] This motive of self-interest perhaps helps to explain why only 20 per cent of DAC bilateral concessionary assistance - was directed to the poorest countries in 1980.[23]

The current recession in OECD countries which some forecasts see as continuing into 1983, combined with attempts in most countries to control public sector expenditures, seem to indicate that prospects for increased real flows of concessional bilateral aid are poor. Pronouncements by officials in the major donor country, the United States, and also in the United Kingdom confirm this pessimism. The OECD itself sees the real rate of growth of all aid at 3 to 4 per cent in the next two or three years, but most of this is likely to be in non-concessional form. In addition to these discouraging forecasts, the general uncertainty concerning future flows of aid from OECD countries is clearly not conducive to proper financial and development planning.

Finally, the fact that much aid is based not on a perceived need but on political, economic and strategic
benefits likely to be derived by donor countries does not
augur well for countries unable to offer such benefits.
Thus while OECD bilateral aid will continue to be the
major source of external funds to the least-developed
countries, its future magnitude and direction are a
source of much uncertainty and concern.

OPEC

Net concessional aid disbursements by OPEC in 1980
totalled about $7 billion of which $6.1 billion was in
the form of bilateral assistance. As a proportion of
GNP, OPEC aid was 1.3 per cent, more than three times as
high as the OECD ratio. However, the major donors:
Saudi Arabia, Kuwait, and the UAE, had ratios of 2.6,
3.8, and 3.9 respectively. Arab countries continued to
receive most of OPEC bilateral aid. In 1980, net disbursements to this group were $4.88 billion out of a
total of $6.1 billion.

Prospects for higher levels of bilateral aid flows,
especially for non-Arab countries, seem poor indeed. The
1980/1981 period might well have been a peak with the
OPEC current account surplus reaching $115 billion in
1980 and about $70 billion in 1981. In 1982 the surplus
is expected to fall to $25 billion and to remain at that
level in 1983, largely as a result of depressed volume
and price factors affecting oil exports.[24]

3. MULTILATERAL INSTITUTIONS:-

The IMF

In late December 1945, 29 Governments signed the
Articles of Agreement of the IMF, setting the institution
into operation. In this post-war period, the Fund set out
to achieve the objectives of exchange rate stability, the
avoidance of competitive depreciations, and the removal or
liberalization of barriers to international trade. Once

these were achieved, it was hoped that the Western industrialized countries would return to enjoying high rates
of trade, investment, and growth on which their economic
revival depended.

In assessing the IMF's role as a source of finance
to developing countries, it is important to note these
objectives which, over the years, have remained largely
intact. Thus, loans to countries for balance of payments
purposes have been granted on condition that barriers to
international trade and payments are reduced or withdrawn.

TABLE 5.3

USE OF IMF'S GENERAL RESOURCES[1] BY NON-OIL LESS-DEVELOPED COUNTRIES

(SDRs Million)

	1970	1975	1980	1981
TOTAL DRAWINGS:	435.5	2474.5	3752.7	7081.7
Western Hemisphere	124.1	610.2	294.4	560.8
Middle East	21.0	190.1	31.6	45.9
Asia	53.5	722.9	1586.6	3299.4
Africa	161.9	465.3	874.1	1875.9
Europe	75.0	486.1	966.0	1299.7
TOTAL REPURCHASES:	730.2	399.5	1860.0	1592.5
Western Hemisphere	300.3	182.1	371.1	274.9
Middle East	9.0	37.0	158.6	153.5
Asia	271.9	105.4	410.7	409.9
Africa	76.2	75.0	494.9	358.3
Europe	72.2	-	424.7	395.8
NET DRAWINGS:	-294.7	2075.0	1892.7	5489.2
Western Hemisphere	-176.7	428.1	- 76.7	285.9
Middle East	12.0	153.1	-127.0	-107.6
Asia	-218.4	617.5	1175.9	2889.5
Africa	85.7	390.3	379.2	1517.6
Europe	2.8	486.1	541.3	903.9

1) Excludes allocation of SDRs, transactions in the Trust Fund and the Subsidy Account, and Gold distributions.

SOURCE: IMF - International Financial Statistics Yearbook 1981, and IFS - July, 1982.

In recent years, most of the institution's lending has
been to non-oil developing countries facing chronic external deficits and requiring serious macroeconomic adjustment measures. From an almost negligible net source of
funds, the IMF, especially in the last two or three years,
has initiated several measures to increase its contribution to the overall financing needs of LDCs.

The IMF was a relatively minor source of external
financing to non-oil LDCs in the period 1973 to 1981. The
annual average net purchases in that period approximated
$1.7 billion, excluding Trust Fund loans. This compares
with an average current account deficit of $49 billion.
Even in the year of peak Fund activity, 1981, net drawings
at about SDRs 5.5 billion, financed only 6 per cent of that
year's aggregate current account deficit. However, simple
averages conceal some of the major contributions of the
Fund at times when external financing was desperately
required by the non-oil LDCs. These were made during the
period 1974 to 1976 when net lending accelerated from minus
SDR 89 million in 1973 to SDR 1980 million in 1976. In
that period, average annual net borrowings from the Fund
equalled about SDRs 1,600 million.[25)]

While there was no net borrowing in the following
three-year period, 1977 to 1979, unprecedented levels of
net disbursements of SDRs 1.9 billion and SDRs 5.5 billion
took place in 1980 and 1981 respectively. When Trust Fund
loans and purchases other than under stand-by and extended
arrangements are included, these levels rise to SDRs 4.2
billion and SDRs 6.4 billion. It seems clear that the
Fund has proved responsive to the financing needs of non-
oil LDCs in the wake of the two oil-crisis periods of
1973/1974 and 1979/1980. In addition, both in terms of
the recent size of its annual net disbursements and of its
efforts at adjustment in those countries experiencing
chronic external payments disequilibria, the institution
cannot be described as an insignificant or negligible

source of assistance to those of its member countries most
in need.

That the Fund has made much progress in its quantitative and qualitative assistance to developing countries
is evidenced by a few observations. Firstly, the institution itself has been concerned about the adequacy of its
loanable funds in meeting the potential needs of members.
As a result, arrangements have been concluded with the
Saudi Arabian Monetary Agency and the Bank for International Settlements for substantial lines of credit to be
made available to the Fund. Secondly, several commentators in OECD countries, and in particular the United
States, have expressed concern that in its heightened
lending activities, the IMF might be relaxing its conditions, especially on such large transactions as the recent
Extended Fund Facility loan to India of SDRs 5 billion.[26]
Finally, developing countries themselves seem far less
strident in their criticisms of the institution than they
were in the early-to mid-1970s.

Partial appeasement of LDCs together with a growing
sense of concern in certain Western Governments that the
IMF is 'going soft' or becoming similar to a foreign aid
agency have resulted from measures by the institution
aimed at facilitating access to its resources. Among the
more important of these are:-

1. The agreement of the Executive Board in
    March 1979, to introduce new guidelines
    on conditionality which by, for example,
    reducing the number of performance cri-
    teria, should facilitate easier access to
    the resources of the Fund.

2. The liberalization of the Compensatory
    Financing Facility (CFF) permitting a mem-
    ber to borrow up to 100 per cent of its
    quota to meet export shortfalls. Pre-
    viously, the limit was 75 per cent of quota

and workers' remittances and tourists'
receipts could not be included in the
calculation of the shortfall. The CFF
was also been expanded in 1981 to compensate for the excess costs of cereal
imports due to temporary, external
factors.

3. The introduction of the Supplementary
   Financing Facility (SFF) which became
   operational in February 1979 to provide
   assistance, in addition to the Fund's
   ordinary resources, to members facing
   balance of payments deficits which are
   large in relation to their quotas, thus
   requiring supplementary resources over
   an extended period of time.

4. The extension of maturities on all IMF
   facilities where conditions may so require.
   In the case of standby arrangements, for
   example, programmes may be extended from
   the usual one-year period to three years,
   while repayment periods on the use of the
   Extended Fund Facility (EFF) may be extended from three to five years, to four to
   ten years.[27)]

5. Introduction of the policy of Enlarged
   Access whereby a country utilizing the
   Extended Fund Facility may draw up to 450
   per cent of its quota over a three-year
   period or up to a limit of 600 per cent of
   quota on the cumulated use of Fund resources.

6. The establishment of the SFF Subsidy Account,
   with the aim of reducing the cost to eligible
   (mostly low-income) borrowers of loans under
   the Supplementary Financing Facility.

Partly under pressure from commercial sources of
finance, the developing countries seem prepared to approach
the Fund more readily than before. While it is too early
to rush to conclusions, it is important to note that
approximately 56 non-oil less-developed countries made
drawings from the Fund in 1981, compared with 37 in 1979.[28]

The role of the IMF in the international monetary system thus depends on whether this trend of larger numbers
of borrowers continues. The Fund commands and has access
to large resources and its ingenuity and flexibility will
be taxed to the limit if it is to cater to the needs of
the LDCs for balance of payments finance while at the same
time maintaining the high level of financial discipline in
its lending policies.

Finally, it must be noted that the IMF also provides
an unconditional, irredeemable reserve asset - the
Special Drawing Right. By means of allocations of this
asset in relation to members' quotas in the Fund, the
institution has so far injected SDRs 60 billion of
liquidity into the international financial system. The
developing countries' share of these assets amount to
SDRs 17 billion or 28 per cent, quite small in relation to
their needs. However, as was noted below, the IMF was not
established to function as a development finance institution and its cool response to demands to link SDR creation
with development assistance must be seen in the light of
the Fund's emphasis on converting the SDR into the world's
principal reserve asset to replace the steadily weakening
dollar. Much effort within the Fund has been devoted
toward this objective, and it is clear that in many
respects, the LDCs' desire to see the issue of SDRs linked
to their development needs is incompatible with the IMF's
wish to develop the instrument into the world's leading
reserve asset.

IBRD

    As the largest source of multilateral finance, the
World Bank and its major affiliate, the International
Development Association (IDA) provided approximately 5 to
6 per cent of net external capital receipts of all
developing countries in the period 1975 to 1980. In
nominal terms, the amounts disbursed have increased from
$0.9 billion in 1970 to $7 billion in 1981.[29]

    In keeping with its objectives of eliminating
poverty and fostering development, the group has generally
allocated about one-third of its loans to agriculture and
rural development. Other major sectors to which loans
have been granted include industry, energy and transportation. Maturities are also development-orientated with
those of Bank loans averaging twenty years, while IDA
concessional credits average fifty years.

    Since the Bank obtains its funds in the international
capital markets,[30] its interest rates on loans are
slightly above market rates. In addition, since the
Bank's creditworthiness in the eyes of the market ulti-
mately depends on the creditworthiness of its borrowers -
its lending is skewed towards the richer of the developing regions such as Asia and the Pacific, Europe, the
Middle East and North Africa, and Latin America. IDA
lending is not subject to such constraints and is available to the poorer nations. But being dependent on
donors' contributions, its funds are limited. So serious
were its funding problems that additional commitments
ceased temporarily in the spring of 1981.

    In order to be of direct benefit to developing
countries, loans committed need to be disbursed. Of the
$12.3 billion committed by the World Bank Group in 1981,
$7 billion was actually disbursed. Bank officials com-
plain several factors are responsible: the absence of
viable projects, the very long time lag between project

preparation and completion (roughly 6 to 10 years), the
lack of skilled personnel in LDCs to manage aspects of the
projects, and also the insufficiency, at times, of funds
to finance the local currency counterpart of a project.
The failures of domestic policy will be discussed in a
later chapter.

With the recent doubling of its capital to $80
billion, the World Bank Group as a development institution
is now better equipped to continue the task of attacking
poverty and stimulating growth in the poorer regions of
the world. To this end, also, an encouraging development
has taken place: the President of the World Bank
announced in 1979 a proposal to increase the volume of
programme lending to countries facing severe balance of
payments problems of a structural nature.[31] Such assistance on normal bank terms of 25-year maturities is most
welcome to these countries. In fiscal 1981 alone, $717
million was approved for structural adjustment loans.

Since, at least for the time being, the supply of
funds to the Bank is no longer a serious problem, it is
for the developing countries themselves to secure access
to these resources by means of prudent economic management.
Table 5.4 below shows some recent trends in World Bank and
IDA lending.

TABLE 5.4

BANK AND IDA: TRENDS IN LENDING, BY SECTOR

(US$ Millions: Fiscal Years)

	1979	1980	1981
Agriculture and Rural Development	2,522	3,458	3,763
Development Finance Companies	591	818	1,113
Education	496	440	735
Energy Oil, Gas, and Coal	112	457	659
Power	1,355	2,392	1,323
Industry[a]	843	423	886
Nonproject and Structural Adjustment	407	522	1,012
Population, Health, and Nutrition	114	143	13
Small-Scale Enterprises	86	260	229
Telecommunications	110	131	329
Transportation	1,904	1,445	1,063
Urbanization	310	349	501
Water Supply and Sewerage	1,019	631	535
Other[b]	143	13	131
TOTAL	10,011	11,482	12,291

NOTE: Details may not add to totals due to rounding

a) Includes nonfuel minerals and mining

b) Includes technical assistance and tourism

SOURCE: World Bank Annual Report - 1981.

4. MINOR SOURCES OF FINANCE:-

These sources are mentioned more for purposes of com-
pleteness than for their importance. Nevertheless, it is
important that developing countries keep all options of
external finance open in considering their foreign
exchange needs.

4.1   Direct Investment Flows

Table 5.1 shows that in percentage terms, this source financed only a small portion (3 per cent) of imports of non-oil LDCs in the period 1973 to 1982. It played virtually no part in financing imports of the least-developed countries. In money terms, net direct investment flows to all non-oil countries increased slowly from an annual average of about $5 billion in the period 1973 to 1977 to an estimated $14 billion in 1982.[32] The low-income countries' share in these flows is esti-mated at approximately $0.3 billion per annum.

Being funds seeking a suitable commercial rate of return direct investments tend to be concentrated in the higher-income LDCs such as Argentina, Brazil, and Mexico in Latin America, and Hong Kong, Malaysia, and Singapore in South East Asia.[33] In many of these countries, direct investment flows have helped to reduce the need for expensive commercial borrowing while at the same time contributing to the growth in export earnings. Malaysia, for example, relies more on direct investment than on bor-rowing for its external financing needs. In the period 1974-1978, 80 per cent of long-term and portfolio invest-ment was provided by direct investors. For similar reasons, Singapore has little need for external borrow-ing.[34]

However, for most LDCs, direct investment will con-tinue to be a minor source of finance as long as they refuse to surrender control over any significant propor-tion of their natural resources and their economies to non-resident investors.

4.2   Suppliers/Exports Credits

OECD data in Table 5.1 show trends in suppliers credits since 1971. In 1980, some 16 per cent of total net receipts were financed from this source. While the table differentiates between private and official cre-dits, increasing amounts of assistance by Governments to

private exporters imply a growing convergence, fuelled by
a mutual interest in higher export earnings. Official
assistance takes the form of both guaranteeing payment for
exports through export credits and guarantee bodies such
as the U.K.'s ECGD and the U.S.'s Ex-Im Bank, and of more
direct financial assistance, including 'mixed credits'
aimed at reducing the overall interest cost to the impor-
ter to rates much below OECD market levels. 'The Economist' estimates that during 1980, 18 per cent of American,
34 per cent of French, 35 per cent of British, and 39 per
cent of Japanese exports received official support.

    While both industrialised and a growing number of
developing countries compete aggressively in using export
credits to win overseas markets, importing LDCs need to be
aware of the disadvantages of excessive reliance on credits as a source of funds. In this context, the experience of Ghana is most instructive.[35] While most useful
as a means of financing urgently-required raw materials
and capital equipment, large-scale contracting of credits
is likely to lead to severe debt-servicing and foreign
exchange problems.

4.3 Bond Markets

    Bonds, issued in foreign currency by countries wish-
ing to borrow overseas[36] are of three main types:

    (i) "Traditional" Foreign Bonds:-
        Fixed-interest securities with maturities
        of up to twenty-five years floated in a
        capital market country such as West Germany,
        Japan, Switzerland, and the U.S.A.

    (ii) Eurobonds:-
        Negotiable, usually fixed-rate securities
        with maturities ranging from seven to fifteen
        years, floated in the euromarkets.

(iii)   Floating Rate Notes:-
Medium-term (five to ten-year) nego-
tiable securities, presently being
issued mostly by international commercial banks as a means of diversifying
their liabilities, but also issued by
Governments and international institutions to investors reluctant to hold
fixed-interest paper in periods of
uncertainty as characterized by high and
rising rates of inflation and interest.
These bonds or notes, therefore, offer
interest rates which fluctuate with market rates, thus offering some protection
or "inflation-proofing" to the investor.

A recent innovation is the "Convertible Floating
Rate Note," where the holder has the option to convert
his floating rate note into a fixed-interest security at
specified times.

The large institutional investors which predominate
on the demand side of the bond markets are attracted to
an issue only where the borrower is regarded as "creditworthy." This means, firstly, that the external borrowing record of the country is good in terms of prompt
interest and principal repayments, that the economy
appears to be well-managed, and that the long-term prospects for the economy are sound so that no financial
problems seem likely to postpone the redemption of the
bonds when they become due. Insurance companies and pen-
sion funds holding large amounts of customers' and
clients' savings will normally be impressed more by the
apparent soundness of the issuer than by higher than
usual yields. Unfortunately, few non-oil LDCs are perceived by long-term portfolio investors as being sound
enough.

Table 5.5 shows that bond markets have been a source of funds only to a relatively small group of non-oil LDCs and that the amounts provided are small in comparison with international lending by commercial banks. Between 1975 and 1981, gross borrowing advanced from $0.7 billion to $3.1 billion. In the same period, borrowing from international banks had risen from $15 billion to $50 billion. Thus, it is estimated that bond issues financed 4 per cent of the combined current account deficit of non-oil LDCs in 1981, while international banks financed almost 50 per cent. Further the non-OPEC LDC share in total bond issues for 1981 was only 7 per cent. In keeping with the rather strict criteria required of borrowers by bondholders, only the richer of the LDCs have obtained, or for that matter, sought, access to the bond markets. In 1978, for example, 5 countries accounted for 58 per cent of total non-oil LDC borrowing from this source: Argentina, Brazil, Malaysia, Panama, and The Philippines.[37] In 1981, 4 countries, Mexico, South Korea, India, and Argentina accounted for almost 80 per cent.

Nevertheless, it must be stated that between 1975 and 1978 the number of non-oil countries gaining access to relatively long-term bond finance has increased from 14 to 28. In 1979 and 1980, the number averaged 20, while in 1981 it reached a low of 15. Recent entries to the market include Bermuda, Costa Rica, Greece, India, Peru, and Thailand. Access has provided a new and important source of finance to these countries.

Prospects for an increased role for bond-market financing in the developing countries have been hit by the uncertainty which prevails over fixed-rate financing given rising inflation and interest rates. Floating-rate issues are thus likely to continue to be as popular with investors as they were in 1981, when 70 per cent of LDC issues took this form. Whether fixed or floating, however, LDCs need to be aware of the advantages of gaining access to

TABLE 5.5

BOND ISSUES BY SELECTED NON-OIL LDCs 1975-1981

(In Millions of US Dollars)

	1975	1976	1977	1978	1979	1980	1981
Argentina	16	–	43	266	417	164	120
Brazil	35	193	856	936	736	316	15
Chile	53	–	–	50	84	82	30
Costa Rica	–	–	–	20	–	109	–
Ecuador	–	–	8	62	–	–	–
Egypt	–	–	–	25	–	–	–
Haiti	–	–	–	–	8	–	–
Hong Kong	25	–	128	–	–	–	50
India	–	–	–	–	–	30	136
Ivory Coast	–	10	–	–	–	14	–
Korea	–	74	72	56	44	48	133
Malaysia	–	10	43	139	152	–	–
Morocco	28	45	28	91	22	23	–
Panama	–	14	27	215	111	25	–
Papua New Guinea	25	–	25	–	–	–	–
Philippines	–	367	130	216	176	67	65
Singapore	12	175	155	25	25	–	–
Thailand	–	–	–	69	176	46	43
Tunisia	–	49	10	26	–	–	–
Yugoslavia	–	90	129	127	96	37	–

Memo Item:

Total Bond Issues of Non-oil LDCs   –   1,915   3,439   4,114   3,120   2,283   3,115

SOURCES: IBRD: Borrowing in International Capital Markets
           (various issues), and OECD: Monthly Financial
           Statistics.

this source of long-term finance, and to devote their
energies to improving the current state and future prospects of their economies, on which such access depends.

4.4   European Investment Bank (EIB)

The EIB was established simultaneously with the creation of the European Economic Community in January 1958
with the objective of stimulating economic activity especially in the poorer member countries. Since that time,
however, and with the growing level of co-operation

between the members of the Community and the developing
countries, the Bank has become a useful, though minor,
source of finance to the LDCs.

Loans are available from the institution's own
resources at interest rates subsidised by the Community,
for project-finance purposes, mostly on a shared basis
with other external lenders. Projects in industry, energy,
and transport have been particularly supported by the
Bank. With respect to the regional distribution of funds,
of the 208.8 million units of account loaned in 1981, just
over two-thirds went to Africa, with one-third to the
Pacific Region.[38]

While the EIB remains a major lender only in Europe
and the Mediterranean, its willingness to participate in
the co-financing of projects could be of much use to LDCs
seeking to maximize access to long-term sources of
finance.

This chapter has examined the major non-banks
sources of external funds to developing countries, and
some important points need to be mentioned by way of conclusion. First, export earnings are, by far, the largest
source of foreign exchange to LDCs. The implication from
this is simply that efforts at increasing the flow of
foreign exchange are likely to be successful only if they
include measures designed to improve net export earnings.
Secondly, for most of the 1970s, international banks have
been the largest source of borrowed funds to LDCs. In
1981, IMF data show that banks provided almost half of
such resources, while official lenders supplied just over
a quarter.[39] While it is true that the poorest countries
rely almost exclusively on official concessional aid, its
unpredictability, tied nature, and political implications
have caused several countries to look to international
banks as the major source of external funds not only for
traditional trade and project financing, but also for
general development and balance of payments purposes. The
following three chapters discuss the role of the banks in
the growth process of LDCs.

6
Banks as a Source of External Finance in Non-Oil LDCs

In the previous chapter, it was noted that the traditional source of funds to developing countries - official aid - was falling in importance to the non-oil developing countries as a group although it continued to provide about 80 per cent of the external financing needs of the low-income subgroup. Tough conditions attached to balance of payments loans granted by the International Monetary Fund, have deterred countries from seeking access until all other sources have been exhausted. The IBRD, while performing an excellent job in the field of development finance, has, in the past, been constrained by a small capital base, and continues to be constrained by difficulties in disbursing its committed funds at a satisfactory rate. Other minor sources of external funds such as direct investment flows, the bond markets, and export credits are either confined only to the richest countries of the group or in the case of export credits may not be suited to the needs of the majority of developing countries.

In the meantime, commercial banks have been lending increasing amounts to developing countries since the early 1970s, to a large extent, filling the gap resulting from inadequate real flows of official finance, in addition to catering to the ever-growing foreign exchange needs of these countries. In Chapter 3, the thesis reviewed the historical development of bank lending to countries. In the current chapter it examines the current importance of bank lending as a source of foreign exchange to LDCs.

The data presented in Appendix Table 1 show that on average between 1973 and 1982 international bank loans financed about 47 per cent of the combined current account deficit of non-oil LDCs. In monetary terms, net long-term funds provided by the banks have risen from $7.1 billion in 1973 to an estimated $37 billion in 1982.[1] This growth is indeed impressive in spite of the fact that the data on which it is based are understated to the extent that unguaranteed public sector loans and private long-term syndicated credits which are not publicized are not all included.[2] Within a relatively short space of time, therefore, the role of banks has been transformed from that of supplying short-term, mainly trade-related finance to that of a major and indispensable source of medium-term external finance for both balance of payments and project financing purposes. In effect, the banks, after a long break commencing with the collapse of the international capital market in 1929, have now firmly re-established themselves as the most important international financial intermediaries channelling capital from surplus to deficit countries and enabling the latter to sustain and even increase their rates of growth of GNP.

The aggregates indicated above show only an overall picture. An analysis of bank lending to the various subgroups of developing countries reveals that in general, bank lending has concentrated on the richer LDCs. For example, of the estimated $50 billion of gross bank lending to non-oil LDCs in 1981, only $1 billion flowed to low-income LDCs. Net oil exporters and major manufactured-goods exporters attracted $20 billion and $24 billion respectively. As a proportion of the low-income LDCs current account deficit, bank lending is estimated to have accounted for only 9 per cent in 1980 and 6 per cent in 1981 after peaking at 26 per cent in 1979. For net oil importers and manufacturers the banks' share in 1981 was approximately 90 per cent and 68 per cent respectively.[3] As the data for 1982 emerge, it seems clear that this trend is continuing with most of the borrowing being undertaken by Brazil, Malaysia and Mexico.

This degree of concentration, however, should not obscure the fact that banks are an important source of funds to several LDCs which are neither net oil exporters nor manufacturers. As at the end of 1981 about 75 LDCs had debts to banks in excess of $100 million.[4] Further, the banks' role in trade financing and short-term balance of payments support, while unpublicised, has been of vital importance to many poorer countries facing liquidity problems.

Much of the current analysis of medium-term euro-currency lending by international banks begins in 1973 with the quadrupling of petroleum prices by OPEC which precipitated the so-called "oil crisis." The large current-account surplus accruing to the OPEC states, a large proportion of which was placed with the big U.S., and European banks, is then "re-cycled" by the banks to oil-importing countries. This analysis, to say the least, is incomplete. While the oil crises may have served to dramatize the need for, and the increased importance of, international financial intermediation, and while the banks' role in "recycling the OPEC surplus" was being much praised and publicized in the financial press during 1973/74, the data available show that bank lending to developing countries was already rapidly accelerating in the 1971/72 period.[5] With high export prices of primary commodities, many LDCs were enjoying, for the first time in many years, a healthy balance of payments position. As a result, many development

projects requiring heavy importation of capital goods
were initiated and the banks were approached to finance
a significant proportion of these. A growing amount of
external deposits could now be lent profitably to seem-
ingly creditworthy borrowers. On the supply side during
this pre-"oil crisis" period, growing central bank
deposits into eurocurrency market banks and relatively
lax monetary policies in especially the United States,
both contributed to the volume of loanable funds available for borrowing by developing countries. Analyses of
demand and supply factors in international bank lending
after the oil price rise in 1973 are numerous and well-
known and need no detailed repetition. The analysis here
would re-emphasize that the oil price rises resulting in
large surpluses to OPEC and equally large deficits in the
rest of the world served only to reinforce the importance
of international financial intermediation in the growth
process of developing countries.

SOME CHARACTERISTICS OF BANK LENDING

Except for small loans of around $10 million, most
lending by banks to developing countries is funded by a
syndicate of banks headed by that bank which was ini-
tially approached and asked to arrange the loan.
Interest rates are quoted as percentages above mostly the
London inter-bank offered rate (LIBOR), but also the New
York or the Japanese prime rate. At present these margins range from 0.25 to 2.5 per cent, with the lower margins being charged to countries regarded as creditworthy.
Maturities range from three to eighteen years depending
on the needs of the borrower and the willingness of the
lender.

In looking at creditworthiness criteria used by
banks in their lending to countries, one is immediately
struck by the similarity to domestic credit assessment.
In lending to a firm a banker looks at such variables as
previous borrowing record and repayment performance,

present and projected levels of debt outstanding and
debt service payments, present levels of earnings, and
projected earnings, out of which repayments must be made.
The banker also tries to determine the ability of the
managers to run the business efficiently over the period
of the loan at least. Finally, he might wish for the
deposit of some form of collateral security or simply a
guarantee from the directors or from another firm. In
country lending "earnings" is replaced by exports and
"managers" by finance and economics ministers, the planning agency, and the central bank. International
bankers will, however, be the first to protest that
country-risk analysis is not as simple as all that.
Deficiencies in economic data, the difficulties inherent
in projecting exports, especially of primary commodities
and metals, and the need to assess political stability
all render the exercise quite complicated. Nevertheless
after many years of experience and with the development
of new and sophisticated country analysis techniques[6]
bankers are now able to refute earlier statements by some
international institutions that bankers are not "qualified" to lend to countries.

For the future, several factors appear to militate
against the continued role of banks in LDC financing.
High real rates of interest in the major capital market
countries are a major issue. In 1981, LIBOR averaged
more than 16.5 per cent, equivalent to 8 per cent in real
terms. It has been estimated that for every 1 per cent
rise in interest rates, some $2 billion is added to LDC
debt servicing.[7] The current recession in OECD countries, political uncertainty in several borrowing countries, and the rising number of actual and proposed debt
rescheduling exercises, all add to some forecasts of a
slowdown of bank lending. The data already available for
1982 appear to confirm these. Compared with the same

period in 1981, bank lending to LDCs slowed considerably
in the first quarter of 1982 in terms of both the value
of loans and the number of borrowers. Notwithstanding
these preliminary figures, the majority of forecasts,
including those of the IMF, the World Bank, and such
respected institutions as Morgan Guaranty and Amex Bank,
predict a continued growth in bank lending to non-oil
LDCs, although at a more modest rate than that of the
late 1970s.[8]

In the light of the concerns mentioned above, and
as the major banks approach existing prudential limits on
lending to individual LDCs, only the more creditworthy
countries are likely to be assured of continued access to
significant amounts of medium-term bank finance. It is
for developing countries to make attempts to meet creditworthiness criteria of the banks in order that such
access be achieved.

TABLE 6.1

SOURCES OF NEW FUNDS IN THE EUROCURRENCY CREDIT MARKET
(US$ billions)

	New Deposits in International Banking Market			
	1980	(%)	1981	(%)
Countries Reporting to the BIS[1]	156.3	(64)	155.6	(65)
Other Developed Countries	5.9	(2)	3.4	(2)
Eastern Europe	0.8	-	0.1	(-)
Major Oil Exporting Countries	41.6	(17)	3.2	(2)
Non-Oil LDCs	4.1	(2)	10.4	(4)
Offshore Banking Centres	27.2	(11)	55.3	(23)
Other	6.7	(3)	10.6	(4)
TOTAL	242.6	(100)	238.6	(100)

1) The Group of Ten Countries and Switzerland, Austria, Denmark and Ireland.

SOURCE: BIS Annual Report 1982

7
The Contribution of International Banking to Growth in Non-Oil Developing Countries

With very few exceptions, writers on the economics of developing countries have tended to ignore the contribution of international banking to the growth performance of these areas in the post-World War II period. Unfortunately, most of the literature on the relationship between the banks and the LDCs seems excessively preoccupied with the negative aspects such as the possibility of overborrowed countries defaulting on their obligations to the banks and the general "dangers" of bank lending.[1] While it is doubtless important to exercise caution in any kind of commercial lending, to emphasize only on the disadvantages of such lending results in a very unbalanced analysis.

The potential of international lending by banks as a source of international liquidity and balance of payments and development finance has long since been recognized by a handful of academic and bank economists. Kindleberger and Meier[2] have already been mentioned in Chapter 2 above as having recognized the importance of international financial intermediation as a means of fostering growth. While international banks were not specifically mentioned and Kindleberger appears to be emphasizing on international long-term capital markets as the first-best mechanism for transferring international savings it is clear that international financial intermediation cannot exclude the role of banks. In addition, Kindleberger stresses the role of intermediation in providing the international liquidity that is necessary to offset fluctuations in export receipts and without which the growth path in LDCs could be erratic with gains achieved in the peaks of foreign exchange receipts being offset by negative growth in the troughs.

While recognizing that the poorest of the LDCs will be unable to gain access to international commercial funds, Diaz-Alejandro regards the benefits of eurocurrency borrowing in terms of increasing the financing options open to developing countries. Especially attractive features of this source are the speed of disbursement of funds once the loan has been finalized and the relative absence of restrictions concerning the use of funds; some countries may use it for boosting reserves, others, for financing medium-term projects. His views on international bank lending may be aptly summed up in this quotation:-

> ...such transactions are carried out in a cold standoffish commercial spirit which contrasts sharply with the tangled, emotional relations surrounding concessional finance. Without dramatics, countries as diverse in their domestic policies as Algeria, Bulgaria, Cuba, Peru, Colombia, Ivory Coast, The Philippines and South Korea have been making quiet deals with the money-lenders and obtaining funds which may be spent, largely on any country and for anything.[3]

Lewis also sees the advantages of borrowing from the banks in terms of a faster rate of disbursement and greater flexibility in use of funds. An important result of this flexibility is that, unlike bi-lateral aid and loans from the multi-lateral financial institutions, funds borrowed from banks may be used to repay older loans.

> Then there is the wonderful banking practice of 'rolling-over' which seems to mean that the loan need never be repaid.[4]

Wellons, [5] in a careful and detailed study intended
to inform policy-makers on the functions and operations of
the eurocurrency market as a source of finance, sets out
generally, and in case studies, the several uses to which
eurocurrency loans have been put by some LDCs, from financing development projects in Indonesia to facilitating
improved external debt and reserve management in Brazil
and Colombia.

Finally, of the bank economists who have contributed
to the positive literature on eurocurrency lending to
LDCs, the most note-worthy, are Friedman, Hang-Shen Cheng,
Nagy, and Sargen. [6] However, since much of their work
can only be found in banking journals, their contributions
have not reached as wide an audience as they deserve.

In this Chapter, a modest attempt is made at expan-
ding on this literature by establishing some links, both
direct and indirect, quantitative and qualitative, between
bank lending to, and growth in, developing countries. The
conclusion reached is that bank lending does contribute to
increasing output and incomes as it has done in the past.

In the previous Chapter, data were quoted showing, in
aggregate terms, the growing reliance of the developing
countries on international banks as a source of external
finance. Table 7.1 shows, in a more disaggregated form,
the amounts of bank lending which have been channelled to
various sub-groups of LDCs during the period 1976 to 1981.
In those six years, some $200 billion (gross) were lent
to all countries for both project finance and general
balance of payments purposes. It is worthy of note that
even for the low-income countries, bank lending averaged
$1 billion per annum and financed 10 per cent of the cur-
rent account deficit. For those countries which are
neither net oil exporters nor major exporters of manufactures, the contribution of the banks was even more
significant.

TABLE 7.1

BANK LENDING TO NON-OIL DEVELOPING COUNTRIES, 1976-81

(In billions of US dollars; and in per cent)

	1976	1977	1978	1979	1980	1981	1976-1981
Bank lending to non-oil developing countries	21	15	25	40	49	50	200
Net oil exporters	6	2	5	10	14	19	56
Major exporters of manufactures	11	6	13	18	23	24	95
Low-income countries	-	-	2	3	1	1	7
Other net oil importers	2	4	9	9	9	7	40
Unallocated	2	3	-4	-	1	-	2
Bank lending as a per cent of aggregate current account deficit	66	50	63	67	57	49	59
Net oil exporters	75	24	59	109	123	90	80
Major exporters of manufactures	92	73	130	82	73	68	86
Low-income countries	-9	6	20	27	9	5	10
Other net oil importers	25	32	68	52	36	22	39

SOURCES: BIS and IMF

At an even more disaggregated level, it might be instructive to list some examples of the type of loans granted by the banks to LDCs in a sample period, 1978/1979.

TABLE 7.2

SELECTED INTERNATIONAL BANK LOANS TO DEVELOPING COUNTRIES
1978 TO SECOND QUARTER 1979

COUNTRY (Borrower)	PURPOSE	AMOUNT (US$ mn)	SPREAD[1] (per cent)	MATURITY (Years)
ANTIGUA	Tourism Development	10	1.0	n.a
BARBADOS	General Development	10	1.375	7
BOTSWANA	Development of Diamond Mine	45	2.0 (average)	7
BRAZIL (State Electricity Co.)	Hydroelectric Expansion Project	400	n.a	13
COLOMBIA	General Development	400	0.625	10
CUBA (Banco Nacional De Cuba)	General Development	41.6[2]	0.7	7
CYPRUS	General Development	40.0	0.875/1.0[3]	7
GHANA (Bank of Ghana)	General Development	21.5	1.5	2
GUINEA (Private Bauxite Co.)	Bauite Development	15	1.875	7
HONG KONG (Mass Transit Railway Corp.)	Construction of Underground Railway	400	1.0	10
INDIA (Mysore Paper Mills)	n.a	35	1.0	7
MADAGASCAR	General Development	29.6	2.0	6

COUNTRY (Borrower)	PURPOSE	AMOUNT (US$ mn)	SPREAD[1] (per cent)	MATURITY (Years)
MALAYSIA	General Development	400	0.75	8
MEXICO (State Electricity Co.)	Electricity Generation	600	n.a	11
MEXICO	Development of Sugar Industry	300	0.875	10
MOROCCO	Development of Phosphate Industry	100	0.875	8
NAURAU (Republic of Naurau Finance Corp.)	General Development	25	1.125	6
SRI LANKA	General Development	50	0.875/1.0	8
SWAZILAND	General Development	28	1.75	7
THAILAND (Siam Cement Co.)	n.a	50	1.125	8
THAILAND (Electricity Generating Authority)	n.a	60	1.0	10
VIET-NAM (Bank for Foreign Trade)	n.a	42.7[4]	1.5/1.625	5

1) Spread denotes the interest rate above interbank or prime rates charged to borrowers.

2) US$ equivalent of ¥10,000 million.

3) Indicates that a 0.875% spread is applicable during part of the loan period, with a 1 per cent spread applicable to the remainder.

4) US$ equivalent of DM 87.7 million.

5) These loans, which are only a small sample of the overall activities of the banks over the past decade, together with the other data above reveal a substantial contribution to the financing of growth in the LDCs.
SOURCE: World Bank: Borrowing in International Capital Markets 1978 and 1979.

INDIRECT CONTRIBUTIONS

From the borrowing country's point of view, much of the attraction of bank finance derives from the flexibility with which it may be applied. With very few exceptions, bilateral aid is tied to specific projects using material and machinery exported from the donor country; at the present time World Bank loans are also being assigned, for the most part to projects. IMF resources may only be used for balance of payments purposes and their availability is conditional on the achievement of certain specified financial targets. By contrast, bank finance remains largely unconditional.

The availability of external finance free from conditions imposed by outside governments or agencies tends to be regarded by those agencies as not being in the interests of the recipient countries. Their preference is clearly for loans to be carefully monitored and supervised by staff of the agency concerned to ensure that the funds are placed to a project or other use approved by the donor. As Diaz-Alejandro notes:-

> Distrust both of LDC ability to manage sensibly their own financial affairs and of competitive international financial markets is not far from the surface.[7]

This attitude is perhaps not surprising when seen in the harsh light of retrospection and experience in some countries which embarked on an import spending spree as a result of the sudden multiplication of their international reserves caused by the commodities booms of 1971/72 and 1973/74 and failed to allocate efficiently, with a view to the uncertain future, a very scarce and valuable resource. "Failed to allocate efficiently," of course, is putting it mildly, outright wastage of foreign-exchange and its investment in ill-advised large-scale projects were common. However, not all LDCs were wasteful, and even those which were unwise, having "burnt their fingers," now treat foreign exchange with much more respect than previously.

The relative unconditional nature of bank finance
can prove beneficial to growth in many respects. The
most important of these are in the fields of reserve and
external debt management. Primary-producing and mineral-
rich economies are subject to shocks of both natural and
market origins. In the first category are drought,
floods, and pests which affect harvests, and in the
latter are the various demand and supply factors which
result in low export prices, smaller levels of export
earnings and a depletion of international reserves.
Access to bank loans on these occasions can help to prevent the growth process from coming to a halt by the provision of tiding-over finance. The Compensatory Financing
Facility of the IMF which was established for this purpose, provided on average SDRs 136.4 million between 1973
and 1975, and in its peak year, 1976, released SDRs 1.9
billion to the non-oil developing countries, with conditions attached. In the five-year period 1977 to 1981,
the annual average was SDRs 700 million.[8] The Managing
Director of the Fund himself stated at UNCTAD V in Manila
that the facility financed only about half of LDCs'
export shortfalls between January 1976 and February 1979.[9]
For those countries with access to bank finance and
unwilling to deflate at a time when the economy was
already under strain, this source provided the remainder
of the shortfall.

The most serious shocks to the world economy, and the
non-oil developing countries in particular, have been the
sharp increases in the price of petroleum. In this situation, the banks have helped to sustain the momentum of
growth by providing the loans necessary to meet resulting
foreign exchange shortages. Even the IMF, generally
opposed to the large volume of bank lending for balance of
payments purposes, has stated that the banks

> ... helped to lighten the effect of the downturn
> in economic activity that was experienced by a
> large number of countries in the period 1974-76.[10]

This book would go further and state that by removing
the need for massive deflation as the only response to
the transfer of purchasing power to OPEC, bank lending
contributed in a major way to the achievement of growth
rates of 5 to 6 per cent in the LDCs in the period
1973-78 without which the world economy would have
suffered a much deeper recession than in fact took place.
As Fishlow notes, if the LDCs had not sustained their
growth rates by borrowing,

> ... the consequences easily would have rivalled
> those of the Great Depression.[11]

Some countries, notably Brazil, have moved beyond the
stage of borrowing for tiding-over purposes and have borrowed in anticipation of shocks.[12] The net cost of this
form of insurance cover is the difference between total
borrowing costs and the interest received from re-depositing the funds. With careful and well-timed borrowing and
re-depositing, the net cost of such an exercise should not
be as high as is often imagined in some LDCs.

For those LDCs which would consider the incurring of
these costs not worthwhile or for those which place a
higher premium on "real" imports than on international
liquidity even in periods of great uncertainty,[13] the
alternative precautionary measure would be to develop a
relationship with the banks such that they may be
approached in time of need. The difficulty here, however,
is that at the time of need, market conditions might render bank finance either unobtainable, or available only
at high cost.

Whether a country borrows in anticipation of foreign
exchange difficulties or obtains access to bank funds in
time of need, bank lending enables the economy to progress more smoothly, stop/go policies and the resulting
waste of resources may be avoided, and stability, that
most elusive objective becomes more attainable.

EXTERNAL DEBT MANAGEMENT

Eurocurrency borrowing enables a more active and efficient form of external debt management than was previously possible in developing countries. Debts to bilateral aid agencies, multilateral financial institutions or to suppliers are in general contracted with little scope for bargaining by the borrower. Access to bank finance provides an alternative to tied aid; it eanables a country's negotiators to shop around in the world markets for the best prices and terms on essential materials and equipment required. This ability to purchase freely can result in substantial savings. The costs of tied aid in terms of scarce foreign exchange have been well documented by several authors, and only a few cases are mentioned here.

Little, Scitovsky, and Scott note that estimates for India of the average excess cost of equipment for twenty sample projects due to the tying of aid, yielded an average excess cost of 49.3 per cent.[14] The three authors also quote estimates made by UNCTAD for Chile, Iran, and Tunisia, which all show that the tying of aid resulted in excess costs of between 10 to 20 per cent.[15] In his study of the costs of tied aid for Pakistan, Ul Haq concludes:

> The overall result is that the weighted average price for these 20 projects comes out to be 51 per cent higher from the tied source compared to the international bids.[16]

And:

> A rough estimate made by the author indicates that, if the entire $500 million foreign assistance that Pakistan is likely to receive during the current year is completely untied, Pakistan should be able to save roughly $60 million by procuring supplies in the international market.[17]

Tendler shows that aid agencies in the U.S. may actually encourage extravagant, foreign-exchange intensive projects, refusing to finance anything but the foreign-exchange

costs of a project. In addition, she highlights the
inflexibility in the use of bilateral aid funds by showing that as at 1974, more than 80 per cent of USAID disbursements were being spent in the U.S.[18] Finally, in
more general terms, Streeten cautions against the inappropriate, costly, and wasteful technology which an over-
dependence on foreign aid can encourage.[19] Cases of
second-hand, faulty, or inappropriate equipment arriving,
working for a few months in perhaps too humid a climate
or on rough dirt roads for which it was not designed, and
then collapsing beyond repair are familiar to technicians
in the developing countries. In the meantime, the loan
from the aid agency is unaffected and remains a burden on
the nation's resources for years to come. Bank borrowing
avoids the need for such equipment to be forced upon LDCs
by bilateral aid donors or suppliers' credits agreements.
It also enables a country to consolidate and refinance
older and costlier debt into a more serviceable package
of cheaper, longer-term obligations.[20] A smaller annual
debt-service burden results, given the same quantity of
outstanding debt, which allows foreign exchange to be
diverted to the more directly productive sectors of the
economy.

Finally, but of special importance to Third World
countries, is Pazos' observation that arms-length,
strictly commercial borrowing may be more politically
acceptable than aid dispensed at the whims and fancies of
the industrialized countries.[21] Especially in a situation where donors seem to be placing greater emphasis on
the strategic and economic importance, and the political
affinity of potential aid recipients, access to bank
borrowing can enhance both economic and political inde-
pendence.

That international bank lending has promoted growth
in the developing countries is difficult to prove in any
usual statistical sense. With external funds flowing

from various sources and with growth being an essentially dynamic process involving numerous domestic and external variables, it is difficult to show that any type of foreign borrowing stimulates growth. For this reason, no statistical analysis is used here. It is hoped that the attempt to establish some direct links together with the other, less direct contributions have served to highlight the actual and potential role of international banking in aiding the growth process in LDCs. In the following Chapter, some criticisms of this role are examined.

8
Some Criticisms of the Role of International Banks in Financing the Non-Oil LDCs

Needless to say, not all commentators share the view that commercial lending is in the best interests of the developing countries. Opposing views fall into two broad groups:

1. Those which state that bank lending in general is inappropriate and unsuited to the needs of the countries, and

2. Those which, while conceding that the banks played a vital role in recycling the OPEC surpluses of 1973-1974, and 1979-1980 propose that their role in balance of payments and general development finance should be reduced and replaced by the IMF, the World Bank, and bilateral aid agencies.

Since the first type of criticism is of fundamental nature, it warrants priority in discussion. The following quotations are representative of many which advocate the unsuitability of bank lending to the LDCs:

1. There is a good deal of evidence that (international capital markets, including bank lending) tend, especially in dealings with developing countries, to take a short-sighted view and to follow waves of fashion. At a particular time, some country, or group of countries, comes to be regarded as "creditworthy" which leads private banks to over-lend ... It will also be noticed that

Eurocurrency lending has been highly concentrated in a few countries and that the
wisdom of the market in selecting countries
and projects for their loans has not always
been borne out by experience (Joshi)[1].

2. There are those who have welcomed this growing recourse to the private capital market
by the developing countries as a desirable
trend. ... I recognize that the Eurocurrency
market has played an important part in giving
the developing countries access to the international capital market to an extent previously
impossible since the end of World War II...

Nevertheless, I see very real risks for the
developing countries in borrowing so heavily
in a market with no overall surveillance to
prevent unsound practices ...

Another basic uncertainty inherent in Eurocurrency funds stems from floating exchange
rates on which those funds are generally
made available to the developing countries.
These constitute too volatile a base on which
to finance long-term industrial and infrastructure projects ...

Eurocurrency loans ... are often made even
without any appraisal of the soundness of
the projects they are intended to finance...
(Gaud)[2].

Finally, the Managing-Director of the IMF has deemed
bank lending to LDCs as

... a costly and ill-adapted way of transferring international savings.[3]

If one were to list the arguments against large-scale
lending by banks to the LDCs, the following would feature
prominently:

1. Medium and long-term lending to countries
   places the entire stability of the international banking system at risk should any
   one major borrower default.

2. The banks are encouraging countries to
   finance their deficits instead of adjusting
   to them by means of demand management.

3. Terms on bank lending are too onerous.
   Interest rates are too high and maturities

too short. These terms cause severe
debt-servicing problems in many countries
and offset any benefits that may accrue
from borrowing.

4. There is too much concentration of lenders
   and borrowers, thus increasing the risk
   that difficulties in any one would endanger
   the banking system.

Each of these points is discussed below.

With respect to (1) the major issue appears to be the
perceived dangers of the banks borrowing short in the eurocurrency markets and lending long to the developing
countries. While the banks have been successfully performing this task of maturity transformation for several
years, many critics view the practice as inherently
unstable and would support the more traditional view that
long-term lending should be funded from long-term deposits.
This concern has been expressed by no less a person than
David Rockefeller, the former Chairman of Chase Manhattan
Bank. He has warned,

> ... the banks cannot continue indefinitely
> to take very short-term money and lend it out
> for long periods of time. We hope that this
> problem will be alleviated to some extent by
> countries in the Middle East agreeing to place
> funds at longer maturity....[4]

Most bankers, however, seem to feel that not only is the
essence of banking - both domestic and international -
that of maturity transformation at which bankers have
proved themselves competent over the years, but also that
the resources available in the largely inter-bank market
for eurocurrencies are so great that no well-respected
bank will be unable to fund its loans to the developing
countries. In addition, the recent agreement among the
central banks of the Group of Ten countries[5] that they
will act as lenders of last resort to international banks
domiciled in their respective countries should have served

to remove any residual anxiety concerning the funding
operations of the banks.[6)]

The second argument, that what is needed in the LDCs
is adjustment to balance of payments deficits instead of
mere financing of the deficits, is perhaps most prevalent
in the IMF.[7)] It states that financing merely postpones
the inevitable adjustment required by an economy facing a
current account deficit and the longer the postponement,
the more drastic will be the eventual corrective measures.

While it is generally accepted that persistent and
worsening current account deficits require adjustments to
demand and supply factors in an economy, some countries
clearly feel that they would prefer to adjust somewhat
more slowly than at the pace normally required by the
Fund under normal standby arrangements. Borrowing from
the banks enables adjustment to take place over a longer
period - between five to fifteen years - and with less
disruption to the economy. Consequently, many developing
countries, having satisfied the banks' borrowing criteria, have understandably chosen this alternative. Much
of the current disagreements between the Fund and its
members concern not only the conditions of borrowing, per
se: demand restraint, devaluation and so on, but very
importantly also, the speed with which a country is
required to complete the adjustment.

Fortunately, some recent measures announced by the
Fund with respect to the liberalization of facilities and
the extension of maturities, seem to indicate that the
institution is moving closer to the LDCs' position on the
appropriate speed of adjustment.

That the terms on bank lending are too burdensome to
the developing countries, causing serious servicing
problems is one of the most popular criticisms. Because
of high rates of interest and relatively short maturities,
borrowing countries are said eventually to face a
"bunching" of foreign liabilities requiring repayment. As

the amount of outstanding debt rises, larger proportions
of export earnings need to be diverted to service it, thus
creating a strain on the balance of payments. A debt
crisis may result, necessitating renegotiation and rescheduling of the debt.

A number of countries have experienced difficulties
with their commercial debt. They include Costa Rica,
Egypt, Jamaica, Nicaragua, Peru, Poland, Sudan, Turkey,
and Zaire.

Except in the cases of Zaire and Poland where the
banks appear to have rushed in to lend without a careful
assessment of the economy,[8] the argument that debt crises
are caused by the burdensome terms of bank lending does
not seem to be well-established. Clearly it is for a
government to decide whether commercial debt is appropriate for its particular needs; if it is not, such loans
should not be incurred. But having decided that commercial borrowing is worthwhile and appropriate for the project or programme to be financed, it is not justifiable,
when repayment becomes due, to complain that the terms
were too onerous. In his study of borrowers in the eurocurrency markets, Wellons concludes that inefficient economic management in general and external debt management
in particular, were responsible for the debt problems
which arose in Zaire.[9]

Analysing the terms themselves, the more appropriate
indicator of the costs of bank lending is not the interest
rates themselves, which are market rates, as in any commercial lending, but the "spreads" over market rates
charged by the banks. These spreads are related to the
perceived risk of the loan and the creditworthiness of the
borrower: the greater the perceived risk or the lower is
the credit standing of the borrower, the larger is the
spread.

Table 8.1 shows the improving spreads which have
been enjoyed by the developing countries. Whereas, in

TABLE 8.1

PERCENTAGE DISTRIBUTION OF SPREADS OVER INTER-BANK RATES
CHARGED TO DEVELOPING-COUNTRY BORROWERS

	1975	1976	1977	1978	1979	1980
Up to 0.500	-	-	-	1	11	16
0.501 to 0.750	-	-	-	15	42	39
0.751 to 1.000	-	-	19	31	27	22
1.001 to 1.250	2	8	13	22	13	10
1.251 to 1.500	36	25	16	17	4	8
1.501 to 1.750	37	32	32	7	2	2
Over 1.750	25	35	20	7	1	4
Unknown	-	-	-	1	-	-

SOURCE: World Bank

1976, all countries were having to pay margins of over 1
per cent, by 1980 the proportion enjoying spreads of 1 per
cent and less, had risen to 77 per cent. Data becoming
available for 1981 indicate that spreads continued to be
favourable for creditworthly LDCs. For 1982, while the
banks appear to be differentiating markedly between prime
and non-prime borrowers, well-managed developing countries
have managed to negotiate favourable spreads. As long as
borrowers seek access to market funds, they will have to
expect to pay market rates. The banks can then only be
accused of charging excessive premiums over those rates;
the data indicate that this accusation is not
well-founded.[10]

With respect to maturities, one cannot contend that
the commercial banks are able to offer maturities com-
parable to those of bilateral aid donors and the international development agencies. However, it is equally
indisputable that the banks have been extending maturities
and are far from being the basically short-term institutions that they are often made out to be. The data in

Table 8.2 show the lengthening trend in maturities offered by the banks. Further, as Friedman has noted, creditworthy borrowers may be able to "rollover" the loan when it becomes due - in fact, extending the maturity.[11] Finally, except for the largest of projects, ten-year money from the banks appear suitable for project-finance in many sectors which contribute to growth in the LDCs.

In conclusion, the criticism that the costs of bank borrowing are too burdensome needs some qualification. It would be more accurate to say that all types of commercial borrowing are expensive in periods of high interest rates. Banks are only one source of such borrowing, others include suppliers' credits, and even World Bank loans are linked to commercial rates. It has been noted that the spreads charged over market interest rates by the banks to LDC borrowers have been so low as to cause much concern with respect to the banks' profitability and capital adequacy. Maturities have been steadily lengthening, and well-managed economies may obtain ten-year money suitable for long-term project financing. It would, therefore, seem to be an exaggeration to characterize the terms of bank lending in general as onerous.

The fourth major concern is that bank lending is dangerously concentrated among a handful of banks and borrowers. At the end of 1977, about three-quarters of total U.S. bank claims on the developing countries were held by ten large banks, and seven countries[12] accounted for over one-half of the debt outstanding to private creditors.[13] The level of concentration by U.S. banks has not changed much since.[14] Data published by Amex Bank show that six Latin American countries[15] accounted for about 55 per cent of total LDC borrowing in the Eurocurrency market, and 32 per cent of all borrowing.[16] In 1981, of total developing-country Eurocredit commitments of $43 billion, 60 per cent was made to Latin America.[17]

It is a fundamental principle of banking and

TABLE 8.2
PERCENTAGE DISTRIBUTION OF MATURITIES ON BANK LOANS TO
DEVELOPING COUNTRIES
(In per cent)

	1976	1977	1978	1979	1980
Over 1 year up to 5 years	57	23	8	10	10
Over 5 years up to 7 years	30	64	27	8	20
Over 7 years up to 10 years	5	9	56	60	64
Over 10 years	-	-	6	18	4
Unknown	9	4	3	5	2

SOURCE: World Bank

insurance that assets should be well diversified, or if
diversification is not possible, should be invested only
in very high quality government or corporate stock. The
principle is that diversification reduces risk. Concern
about the concentration of bank lending among too small a
group of countries, therefore, turns on whether those
countries are regarded as good risks. A closer examination of the data on the Latin American countries shows
that of the $182,681 million outstanding to the banks as
at end-1981, some 82 per cent was taken up by four
countries, Argentina, Brazil, Mexico and Venezuela. However, after netting-off of deposits with the banks, the
outstanding amount falls to $108.4 billion. Of this
amount the two major oil producers, Mexico and Venezuela,
account for $47 billion, or 43 per cent. While it is con-
ceivable that these countries might face temporary
liquidity problems, it is unlikely that they will be
unable to service their debts over an extended period.
Similarly, while Brazil and Argentina are presently facing
heavy debt burdens, these are unlikely to persist beyond
the short-term. What has been happening is that banks
have been approaching their own prudential limits on

lending to individual countries. It was reported since
1979 that one American bank had already reached
legally-imposed lending limits on such a borrower.[18] As
the banks near other country limits, the pace of lending
is expected to slacken and appears already to be doing so
as figures emerge for 1982.

In concentrating attention on the larger borrowers,
it is often forgotten that many smaller countries have
benefited from access to bank borrowing. The number of
developing countries borrowing from the banks has
increased from 40 in 1975 to about 60 in 1978, and as at
mid-1981, some 75 LDCs had debts to banks in excess of
$100 million. States as diverse as Antigua, Barbados,
Botswana, The Congo, Fiji, The Ivory Coast, Jamaica,
Mauritania, Mauritius, Papua New Guinea, Senegal and Sri
Lanka have borrowed funds ranging from $10 to $270
million.[19] In conclusion, while the banks themselves
have recognized the problem of concentration, they appear
prepared not to exceed the prudential limits on lending to
any single country, however, in advocating caution against
excessive concentration, it must be borne in mind that
several small countries have also obtained often substantial amounts of finance from the banks.

So far, the book has dealt with some fundamental
criticisms of banks as an appropriate source of finance to
the developing countries. It now proceeds to the second
type of criticism which states that while the banks were
crucial instruments in solving the crisis caused by the
OPEC surpluses of 1973/1974 and 1979/1980, their role of
providing medium-term finance to the LDCs should now be
reduced in favour of the IMF, the World Bank, and bilateral aid agencies. This view is very influential since
it is shared by many commercial and central bankers,
international institutions, and many developing countries.
Arthur Burns, for example, has stated:

> ... with many countries now heavily burdened
> with debt, bankers generally recognize that
> prudence demands moderation ... For that
> reason, they understandably wish to see an
> increase in the relative volume of official
> financial support to countries that continue
> to have large borrowing needs.[20]

The Governor of the Bank of England concurs:

> We should be looking for an increasing role
> for official finance, especially from the IMF,
> to help guide deficit countries towards
> adjustment ... and we may look to some move-
> ment by the banks back towards their more tra-
> ditional role of concentrating on specific com-
> mercial, rather than balance of payments lending.[21]

Finally, Morse, an influential British banker
remarks:

> ... I believe that the change in the pattern
> of development financing has swung far enough
> in the direction of commercial bank lending
> and that official sources should provide a
> larger part of the increase in developing
> country finance.[22]

A return to a more active role by the Fund, a
greater volume of programme-lending by the World Bank, and
larger flows of bilateral aid would all be welcome
developments by easing the pressure on the banks. The
numerous calls for a greater role of official finance is,
therefore, less a criticism of the role of the banks than
an acknowledgment that they alone cannot be expected to
carry the brunt of the task of re-channelling international savings indefinitely. It is now up to the official
institutions to meet this challenge and to share this
task, the efficient execution of which is vital for the
maintenance of international monetary order.

In the discussion above, it was noted that some criticisms levelled against bank lending should more properly
be made against economic policy-making and external debt
management in the developing countries. Chapter 9, therefore, discusses how efficient economic management in the
LDCs can complement international bank lending and so
maximise the benefits accruing from such external flows.

9
The Importance of Appropriate Domestic Economic Policies in Complementing the Contribution of the International Banks

In the post-war preoccupation with balance of payments problems, "gap analysis," and import bottlenecks, the importance of appropriate domestic policy formulation may have become a neglected area in the field of development economics. The general consensus in those early years appeared to be that the developing countries faced a capital shortage which impeded the process of growth. The solution to this problem seemed to lie in the provision of large flows of financial, material, and technical aid. As a result, in the developed countries, aid agencies were established to carry out the development assistance objectives of their respective governments, while in the LDCs, much policy effort was devoted to justifying the need for foreign aid. As Myint notes concerning development economics:

> The subject still gives the impression of having been written up originally to make a persuasive case for increasing international aid to the underdeveloped countries.[1]

In addition, domestic policy-making was influenced by the notion that "orthodox" economics was not relevant to the developing countries, being developed by economists from the industrial countries to analyze the workings of a modern manufacturing economy.[2] It is not surprising, therefore, that given their heavy dependence on exports for earnings and imports for essential materials and

equipment, that policy concern focussed primarily on the
balance of payments on current account and on means of
financing the frequent deficits. To a large extent, this
one-sided concern still persists in many developing
countries.

In the burgeoning literature on the economics of
developing countries, many theoretical and empirical
writings have stressed that domestic policy initiatives
and internal forces are more important than external
factors in providing a framework conducive to growth.[3]
Only two of these are quoted here. Sunkel, for example,
asserts that:

> A nation must use its traditions, culture,
> values, institutions and history to create
> and achieve its own process of development
> and national realization.[4]

While Mikesell's analysis leads him to conclude:

> By and large, countries that are not making
> satisfactory progress, regardless of their
> per capita income, have failed to realize
> the potential returns from their own resources.
> What is required are policies and programs for
> mobilizing, adapting, and reallocating these
> resources, including the training of human
> resources for the operations of a modern
> economy. [5]

These factors will be discussed shortly, but first, it
seems appropriate to note, in broad terms the merits of
a continuous search for appropriate domestic policies
conducive to the achievement of stable growth in a
developing economy.

Firstly, continuous attention to alternative policy
measures encourages rigorous economic research and analysis into the workings of the growing economy. Such
research is useful in challenging, confirming, or reject-
ing long-established "hunches" and rules of thumb which
would prevail in its absence. As a result, much loose
thinking and fallacious reasoning concerning essential
relationships between crucial variables within the

economy, which, unchallenged, could well result in the
adoption of inappropriate and wasteful policies, may be
avoided. The importance of ongoing research in LDCs has
been emphasized by, among others, Bhagwati and Desai,[6]
Brimmer,[7] and Helleiner.[8]

Secondly, a switch in emphasis from external financing
to domestic policy-making as a means of promoting growth
inculcates the spirit of "self-reliance" to which many
countries aspire. Thirdly, constant attention to possible
policy measures permits a poor country to anticipate and
prepare contingency plans for any shocks to which it may
become subject. Disruptions to the economy may thus be
minimized.

In many LDCs, the complaint often heard is that
external factors beyond the control of the policy-makers
cause balance of payments problems and cripple prospects
for growth. While external factors do seriously affect
the balance of payments, it does not necessarily follow
that since the disturbances originate overseas, the
problem is beyond solving by domestic means. Reserve
management, external borrowing, and exchange-rate policies, individually, or in combination, can reduce the
amount of disruption caused and are all under the discre-
tion of domestic policy-makers. Finally, the adoption of
appropriate policy-measures resulting in more efficient
management of the economy improves the credit-rating of a
country, enabling it to gain initial or improved access to
private sources of finance, including commercial banks.[9]
This list is by no means exhaustive but it serves to
emphasize that policy-making, properly designed and
effected, can do much to improve the growth prospects of
the developing countries. The most appropriate premise on
which policy-making may be based is that the pool of
resources available to the country is limited, thus
requiring careful management of all, but especially of
human and foreign exchange resources.

The question of what policies should be adopted
depends on the objectives sought by governments. Some
writers have expressed much cynicism concerning these
objectives. Macbean and Balasubramanyam, for example,
state:

> If an all-out pursuit of economic improvement
> for the mass of their citizens were their real
> goal, governments would not build up defence
> forces to strengths well beyond those necessary
> to meet any likely threat to their territorial
> integrity or other major economic interests.
> They would not invest large sums of money in
> prestigous national airlines and international
> airports which involve them in a constant drain
> on resources to subsidise their loss-making
> operations. They would not set up heavy indus-
> tries destined to run at low capacity for lack
> of customers and requiring endless hefty sub-
> sidies. They would not permit the continuation
> of income differentials set by the colonial
> regimes which place the higher civil service and
> professional classes on a completely different
> income plance from the rural and urban masses.
> They would not allow their national resources to
> be squandered on the importation of expensive
> foreign wine, cars and processed foods for the
> sole benefit of the favoured social groups: the
> politicians, civil servants, military officers,
> and upper business class...10)

Nevertheless, in most LDCs the stated objectives of
governments normally centre on the search for stable and
equitable growth. It is, therefore, the function of
policy-makers to design, and to persuade governments to
implement, those policies which are most conducive to the
achievement of those objectives. Since this book is concerned with the benefits of bank lending to the LDCs, the
emphasis in the Chapter will be on those policies which
best complement and assist in maximizing those benefits.

1. External Debt and Reserve Management

The most direct means of maximizing the effects of
external borrowing is to ensure that the funds are efficiently utilized. In the case of self-financed projects,
the lender will attempt to ensure that this criterion is

satisfied. The problem arises when loans are for
non-self-financing projects and for general development
purposes. Since several potential projects will be competing for the use of external funds, it would be useful
for adequate criteria to be established to govern the
allocation. Of course, each government has its own priorities and it is therefore imprudent to generalize on
what such priorities should be.[11] At this point it is
sufficient to say that whatever the priorities, severe
debt-servicing problems are likely to arise in the
absence of a proper appreciation of the scarcity of
foreign exchange and the high cost of borrowing commer-
cially.

Less direct, but no less important in ensuring that
the benefits from external borrowing are not diluted, is
the need in LDCs for efficient management of international
reserves and the external debt. It was noted in Chapter 8
that some of the disadvantages attributed to bank financing were more due to management deficiencies in the borrowing countries themselves.

Major aspects of an effective debt management system
will normally include:

    (i) the existence of a central agency for
        negotiating and approving external loan
        contracts, and allocating the funds to
        the most efficient uses.

   (ii) Ensuring that the costs and maturities of
        loans contracted are such that they would
        not cause serious debt-service problems;
        for example, the excessive use of short-term
        credits would be avoided.

 (iii) Constant monitoring of the use of the funds
        in the public and private sectors.

  (iv) Co-operation with the central bank, in
        ensuring that reserves are always available
        for servicing the debts as payments become

due. This is most essential, since few
events are likely to damage a country's
standing in the international financial
community more than a failure to meet
debt-service payments on time.

(v) The closest possible monitoring of the
international financial markets so that
borrowings are timed, whenever possible,
to take advantage of market conditions.

(vi) Finally, and most importantly, competent
staff need to be recruited and trained
for carrying out the functions mentioned
above.

With respect to the management of international
reserves, provision for the prompt settlement of
debt-service payments is only part of a more general
responsibility to have ample liquid resources, or access
to liquid resources to meet all urgent foreign currency
requirements - thus avoiding foreign-exchange crises and
all the attendant damage to the economy that would result
from such an event. The benefits of an adequate level of
international liquidity as advocated by Kindleberger,
have already been noted in Chapter 2 in the context of
international financial intermediation. In the context
of the vital link between reserves and external debt, it
is noteworthy that Green, who has had much experience
with this link in the developing countries, should state:

> Strategy on exchange rates, reserve management,
> foreign resource procurement terms and debt-ser-
> vice levels should be relatively insurance - (as
> opposed to Monte Carlo -) oriented. The risks of
> an overtly gambling strategy are high and the
> possible losses outweigh the possible gains, as
> can be seen in the Ghanian, Chilean, and Indonesian
> experiences.[12]

Many borrowers have moved to establish centralized
debt-control systems.[13] Others are slowly being persuaded of the need for such a system, partly as a result

of foreign-exchange problems and/or IMF pressure. Further, some LDCs have been hiring specialist banks and other financial institutions to assist with their foreign-reserve management and external borrowing.[14]

Although very belated, this increased awareness that external debt and reserve management are not mere residual matters of policy but are of primary importance in smoothing out the path of growth and development by ensuring adequate supplies of international liquidity, is a welcome development. It lays the basis for a more efficient use of foreign exchange, over and above the usual exchange control mechanisms, and helps to ensure that external borrowing, once contracted, is put to effective use.

The damage to an economy that results from an insufficient attention to external debt and reserves can be expressed not only in terms of the loss of creditworthiness, which is damaging enough to a country's prestige and self-esteem, but also in terms of a heavy additional foreign exchange burden. Islam notes that as a result of rescheduling operations in four countries, debt-service burdens were increased by fairly large amounts: Argentina's debt-burden rose by $98 million, that of Brazil advanced by $138 million, while for Ghana and Indonesia the increments were $97 million and $117 million respectively.[15] Therefore, while rescheduling may ease the debt-service burden in the short-run, its long-run effects often result in a serious additional drain of the borrower's scarce reserves.

2. The Exchange Rate

A key element in a policy designed to ensure that borrowed funds are effectively utilized is for the price of foreign exchange to be set at a realistic level. Too low a price (an overvalued exchange rate) renders imported goods and services, external borrowing, and foreign exchange in general, cheap options, thus encouraging their

excessive use. Nevertheless, for various reasons,
policy-makers in the developing countries appear most
reluctant to consider exchange rate adjustment as part of
a set of measures to strengthen the external sector by
encouraging exports and by discouraging inessential
imports and excessive external borrowing.

Feelings about exchange rates run very high in some
developing countries. Not only is the rate the price of
foreign exchange; it is also often seen as the symbol of
economic stability and of the prestige of the nation. In
negotiations with the IMF, for example, on the use of its
facilities, often the most contentious issue is the
refusal of a country to devalue its currency on the Fund's
advice. The exchange rate is a non-negotiable subject, as
if a devaluation were a public acknowledgment of economic
failure or political weakness. The almost religious
attachment to fixed exchange rates has been supported by
economic arguments. In the first place, it is persua-
sively argued that the demand for imports and exports in
LDCs is highly inelastic - imports, because they comprise
mostly food, essential spare parts and machinery, and
exports, because a lower price cannot guarantee higher
sales in the highly controlled markets for agricultural
exports such as sugar, coffee, cocoa, and tea. Consequently, the trade gap may not be reduced, and, in fact,
may increase as a result of devaluation.[16]

Secondly, governments point to the possible inflationary effects of devaluation: commodies which are
imported, or which require imported inputs in their manufacture would all be more costly to consumers. Finally,
because of the lag in the effect of devaluation on the
balance of payments, it is not a suitable tool for dealing
with the serious foreign exchange problems faced by
countries. In summary, the LDCs' argument against devaluation centres around its ineffectiveness and its inflationary aspect.[17]

However, in seeking to justify their reluctance to
adjust the price of foreign exchange in the face of
balance of payments problems, the developing countries
neglect the advantages to be derived from a willingness to
adjust. One of the most important of these advantages is
the positive effect on non-traditional exports. An overvalued exchange rate discourages production for export
since firstly, import-substitution industries appear much
more lucrative on account of the ready availability of
cheap foreign exchange to purchase imported inputs and of
government support for such activities. Secondly, a
fixed exchange rate in the face of rising domestic costs
squeezes the profitability of export activities. An overvalued exchange rate is, therefore, a signal to manufacturers and entrepreneurs that import-substitution is a
preferred activity vis-a-vis export-promotion. The many
studies of foreign-trade regimes in developing countries
undertaken by the World Bank, the OECD, and the National
Bureau of Economic Research of the U.S.A., all point to
favourable effects of exchange rate adjustments on
exports.[18] Little, Scitovsky, and Scott's study for the
OECD, for example, shows that:

> There is no doubt that both production for
> export and export earnings respond favourably
> to changes in exchange rates, provided only
> that internal costs do not wipe out the
> increased profitability of exporting.[19]

Similarly, Bhagwati and Srinivasan note the existence of
much evidence in NBER studies

> ... of the responsiveness of minor exports in
> particular and manufactured exports in general...

to price changes.[20] Of course, price incentives may be
provided to exporters without having to devalue the currency. However, where production is geared mainly towards
exports, it is exchange rate policy that can provide
either the major encouragement or the main disincentive.
This comment from the President of the Inter-American

Development Bank serves to underline the importance of
avoiding the temptation to maintain overvalued exchange
rates:

> I want to particularly emphasize the need to
> apply an exchange-rate policy that avoids the
> over-valuation of our currencies, a factor
> that in the past has frequently prejudiced
> the development of Latin American exports.[21]

For the reasons mentioned above, and in spite of the
growing evidence that exchange rate adjustments in
response to domestic inflationary pressures stimulate
export activity, which, in turn, stimulates growth,
authorities in the LDCs remain most reluctant to include
the exchange rate among their policy options.[22] Instead,
direct controls have been perceived as a much more effective means of dealing with balance of payments problems .
However, as the studies on the foreign-trade regimes of
developing countries show, this alternative has not only
failed to have the desired result of reducing the current
account deficits, but worse, has caused much disruption
and waste of resources. Because of the detailed analysis
of the effects of foreign-exchange controls available in
these studies,[23] this Chapter deals only with those
aspects of control which can directly offset the benefits
to be derived from borrowing from the international commercial banks. It, therefore, examines the effects of
direct controls on the use of foreign-exchange, on
exports, and generally, on growth.

When direct controls are adopted as an alternative
to devaluation, the official price of foreign exchange
remains unchanged while its allocation is determined by
the exchange control authority. Allocations are normally
granted on the basis of the "essentiality" of the import,
with food, fuel, raw materials for industry, spare parts
and "essential" machinery being priority items in the
merchandise account, and with debt service payments as
the most important item of the services account. However,

in addition to determining what items should be given priority, the authority must also decide which firms or industries should receive allocations of foreign exchange and in what quantities. It can, therefore, to a large extent, determine which firms should prosper (by being granted foreign-exchange allocations) and which should decline or be put out of business (by being denied allocations).

The former group is the major beneficiary of a system of direct controls, enjoying preferential access to cheap supplies of foreign exchange. As a result, the members of this group may not always be as appreciative of the scarcity of foreign exchange as is warranted by the balance of payments position, and may thus treat foreign exchange as a cheap and plentiful resource. While the control authority may decide which firm or sector should have access to imports, it does not necessarily cause an increase in the efficiency with which foreign exchange is used. As Leith notes in his study of Ghana:

> The non-price rationing of the import-licensing
> system and the segmented capital market were
> employed by the policy-makers to ensure that
> particular activities were favoured in the
> allocation of capital and of licences for imported
> materials.... Yet output and employment did not
> respond as they 'should' have to this generous
> treatment. Why? The answer lies in large part
> with the signals individuals received from the
> allocative system: cheap and relatively plentiful
> supplies of capital and imported materials for the
> favoured ones. The response was to treat them as
> cheap and plentiful. [24]

Since the subsidy implicit in an overvalued exchange rate accrues mainly to urban-based importers, manufacturers, and their employees, while the rural-based producers of primary products for export suffer an implicit tax, Lipton argues that the net effect is a massive transfer of wealth from the rural to the urban areas - further reducing the agricultural base that is so important in a developing country endowed with mainly land and

labour.[25] In support of this thesis he notes that in
Argentina, just before the 1959 devaluation, $500 million
were being transferred annually from the agricultural to
other sectors of the economy, because of the overvalued
rate.[26]

Finally, Weisskopf, in concurring with the damaging
effect on agriculture which an overvalued exchange rate
can engender, is also in broad agreement with Leith in
arguing:

> Government rationing of capital and foreign
> exchange often allows the most influential
> firms to obtain these factors at a relatively
> low price and thereby permits high profits
> while encouraging low priority use of scarce
> factors.[27]

Direct controls as an alternative to the proper
pricing of foreign exchange may also result in waste and
inefficiency with respect to both domestic and foreign
resources on account of the frequent shortages of food-
stuffs, raw materials, and spare parts for machinery.
These shortages are caused by delays in issuing licences
and foreign exchange permits and their costs in terms of
lost output and exports serve only to worsen an already
weak economy.[28] Costs of delays may also be counted in
terms of additional interest which accumulates the longer
payment of invoices is postponed beyond their due dates.
In addition, suppliers anticipating delays, may add their
own premia to invoice amounts to compensate for those
delays. Further, importers have been known to over-order
supplies in anticipation of delays in the approval of
import and foreign exchange permits.[29] This practice
results in the wasteful locking-up of scarce foreign
exchange at the same time as other, more pressing needs
for essential items remain unmet. Finally, those indi-
viduals and businesses not fortunate enough to enjoy
access to official sources of foreign exchange become
willing customers in the black-market for foreign currency

that seems always to accompany a regime of direct controls. The black-market price is an indication of the value attached to foreign currency by buyers and sellers in the market. Quite apart from the huge profits obtained by sellers in the market, large amounts of foreign exchange are denied to the economy. Instead of depending on the police to solve what is essentially an economic problem, consideration needs to be given to adjusting the exchange rate to a level sufficient to remove the incentive for black-marketeering and to ensure that all flows of foreign exchange accrue to the central bank and the commercial banks where they can supplement the resources available to the economy.

Even on this brief examination of the consequences of an overvalued exchange rate coupled with comprehensive controls over the use of foreign exchange, it seems clear that the enthusiasm often expressed in favour of such a policy is somewhat unwarranted. It may lead to a wastage of existing stocks of foreign exchange, discriminates against agriculture and has adverse effects on growth without achieving the desired objective of reducing the deficit on the balance of payments.[30] It is therefore not surprising that those countries which seem to have benefited most from external borrowing have been careful to avoid an overvaluation of their currencies. As a result, their export growth has remained vibrant and their GDP growth has been maintained. Exchange rate policy is thus a vital complement to external borrowing, if the resulting inflows are to be utilized as efficiently as possible.

The policies mentioned above may be considered as being directly related to improving the efficiency with which foreign-exchange resources are allocated and utilized. Policies related to the external debt, the balance of payments and the exchange rate, however, need to be

complemented with other domestic measures if the economy
is to benefit fully from external capital flows. The
most important of these concern financial policy and the
management of the public sector. The former, on account
of its potential for increasing the level of domestic
savings thus minimizing the need for external borrowing,
and the latter because of the growing tendency in
developing countries for state-owned corporations to control large proportions of the economy's resources.

3. The Domestic Banking and Financial System

Once the process of growth is seen as one in which
resources are channelled from savings into activities
that contribute to output and incomes, the importance of
developing an efficient domestic financial system becomes
clear. While, as noted in Chapter 2, the writings of
Goldsmith, Shaw, McKinnon[31] and others have all shown
the theoretical justification for effective financial
intermediation as the basis of a "self-reliant" approach
to economic growth, and while empirical evidence of its
contribution to growth in many countries is available,
monetary and financial policy in many LDCs is still
characterized by banking systems which remain passive
collectors of savings and very conservative in their
lending policies. Low nominal, and negative real
interest rates effectively penalize savers and subsidize
borrowers. As in the case of foreign-exchange, therefore, borrowers are encouraged to view the banking system
as a cheap source of working capital with little incentive to utilize the funds along efficiency criteria.[32]

A first priority, therefore, for the establishment
of a strong domestic economic base would be to revitalize
the financial system by encouraging the banks to be more
aggressive in seeking savings and lending opportunities,
and by rewarding savers and pricing loans at interest
rates which are at least higher than current rates of
inflation. The lack of enthusiasm for an active banking

and interest rate policy in LDCs originates from two
opposite quarters. It is either contended that some
countries are so poor as to be unable to save to any
marked extent, or that because of the absence of suitable
lending opportunities, the banks have a limited role to
play. It might be added that a third reason often
advanced is that the tax system is a more efficient
mechanism for acquiring domestic resources than the banking system.[33]

With respect to the first contention, it might be
more accurate to say that only a small proportion of
domestic savings are held with the institutions from
which statistics are collected. Either because of
unfamiliarity with, or lack of confidence in, existing
savings institutions, many people choose to place their
surplus funds in cattle, land, or in gold and other precious metals. The myth that peasants and small farmers
do not save is being exploded by studies which show some
surprising results. Lipton, for example, quotes evidence
indicating that small farmers in West Pakistan were
saving up to 12 and 13 per cent of their incomes in the
period 1964-5; savings rates of 15 per cent were achieved
by Thai farmers in 1963, while those of India achieved 5
to 8 per cent in the period 1967-8.[34] Since the potential for savings does exist, banking systems would do well
to extend the savings network into rural areas,[35] paying
attractive interest rates and inspiring confidence in the
savings institutions either by means of government
guarantees to savers or by slowly building customer confidence in the soundness of the banks and in the integrity
of the managers.

With respect to the second contention that there are
no suitable lending opportunities into which savings can
be channelled, this is a reflection of the need to change
the institutional structure of the financial system,
perhaps incorporating the establishment of long-term

lending agencies. Indeed, it is indicative of a distorted financial system that banks are swamped with liquidity while at the same time the government is negotiating with aid agencies for foreign and local currency financing of investment projects. An efficient banking system is, therefore, an essential complement to external borrowing not only because it enables efficient accumulation and allocation of domestic savings, but also since it can act to reduce dependence on foreign borrowing by substituting domestic resources whenever possible. By so doing, foreign exchange may be diverted to the more deserving activities.

4. Public Sector Management

In those developing countries with a large public sector, access to international bank finance is enhanced by efforts to mould the sector into a set of well-managed and profit-making enterprises. Given the shortage of skills available, this task would be difficult, yet, it must be tackled seriously if the public sector is to make any real and lasting contribution to the economy. Basch has presented an interesting set of criteria for assessing the performance of state-owned enterprises:

> Do these enterprises contribute to the budget at least such amounts as would be obtained through taxation were they privately owned? Moreover, do they generate profit commensurable with profits of similar private enterprises, and do they provide for adequate depreciation and retain earnings for additional investment? (If not) It becomes clear that they do not contribute as much to the capital formation of the economy as could reasonably be expected from similar private enterprise.[36]

Further, the World Bank notes:

> In countries where government-owned manufacturing enterprises are important, there is a clear need for greater cost-consciousness, autonomy, and accountability among managers.[37]

The importance of efficient management can hardly be overestimated. With respect to gaining access to bank

borrowing it is perhaps the most vital consideration. A
noted expert on development finance, now at one of the
major financial institutions remarks:

> This relation of individual borrowing to general
> economic management is the key to understanding
> the great differences found in the ability of
> developing countries to find access to private
> credit markets.[38]

Two other bankers, in assessing factors which are important in deciding whether to lend to a developing country,
are of the opinion that

> The analysis of public policy is almost always
> the key to country credit analysis.[39]

With respect to economic growth, management is
equally crucial. The World Bank, in its 1979 Annual
Report, states that in East Africa, foreign exchange is
scarce, not only because the region faces adverse terms of
trade, but also on account of

> ... persistent structural problems and con-
> tinuing weaknesses in economic management,
> both of which have made diversification in
> production and exports difficult to achieve.[40]

The situation is made worse by emigration which results in
managers being in short supply. Myint attributes better
performance of the economies of Malaya, the Philippines,
and Thailand as against Burma and Indonesia in the 1960s
to more effective economic policies and better management.[41] In looking at the growth performance of the
developing countries, it appears that it has been those
countries which seem to be better managed that have
enjoyed higher growth rates and greater access to private
banks and other sources of external finance. The conclusion is clear: growth depends in large measure, on having
access to external financing. Access to the largest
single source - the banks, will be enhanced to the extent
that by means of appropriate economic policies and effective economic management, the country is seen to be making
serious efforts towards the objective of stable growth.

Many developing countries now facing economic stagnation,
can, by means of adopting a more aggressive stand toward
policy-making, not only help themselves out of the current
depression, but also open doors to sources of medium and
long-term finance that were previously closed to them. To
quote Friedman once more:

> As the recent experience of India indicates,
> even countries with a past history of sluggish-
> ness in economic growth and in export of manu-
> factures are now able through appropriate policy
> measures to achieve rapid increases in exports
> and debt-servicing capacity and to lay the basis
> for enhancing their credit-worthiness with pri-
> vate banks.[42)

This Chapter has attempted to underline the importance of domestic policies in complementing the contribution of international bank lending to growth in the
LDCs. The policies mentioned above are by no means comprehensive.[43) Nevertheless, it is hoped that, at least,
the propositions that external borrowing cannot be a sub-
stitute for domestic action and that in the absence of a
healthy domestic economic framework the benefits from borrowing will be greatly diluted, have been accepted.

For the poorest of the developing countries, neither
the best of domestic policies nor access to bank finance
is sufficient to relieve the high incidence of poverty.
Given the present inadequacy of incomes and domestic
resources, large flows of long-term concessional aid will
be required if even the basic needs of the people are to
be met. The following Chapter turns to these special
financing needs of the poorest LDCs and looks at some proposals for meeting them.

10
The Financing Needs of the Least-Developed Countries

While banks have extended loans to several countries classified as the "least-developed"[1] of LDCs, their aggregate contribution to the external financing of this sub-group has been small, amounting to only $1 billion of the $50 billion borrowed by all non-oil LDCs in 1981. The banks have not contributed significantly to economic progress in these countries for two basic reasons. Firstly, from the point of view of the banks themselves, this group of roughly forty countries are too poor to afford the cost of bank loans. Their foreign-exchange earnings are hardly sufficient to buy the essential items required and would be clearly inadequate to service any large amounts of commercial debt. In summary, banks, as trustees of their depositors' funds, regard large-scale lending to the poorest countries as too risky.

From the point of view of the countries, medium-term, funds at market rates are not appropriate to their needs. For the kind of investments required and the resources available, long-term, concessional finance obtainable from bilateral and multilateral sources is the preferred option. Such finance provides more than 80 per cent of the external funds flowing into the sub-group.[2] Given the common characteristics in these countries of low incomes, the scarcity of basic needs like food, potable water, shelter, and education, and the general incidence of poverty,[3] the financial needs of the least-developed countries are indeed enormous.

Various estimates by UNCTAD and the World Bank put the financial requirements of these countries at between $30 to $45 billion per annum if basic needs are to be adequately provided, and if growth of 3 to 4 per cent is to be achieved.[4]

Compared with existing concessional flows to the poor countries, the achievement of this target seems highly unlikely. OECD data show that net flows of official grants and concessional loans to all developing countries amounted to $33 billion in 1980 of which $14 billion went to low-income countries.[5] Projections show this amount rising to no more than between 5 to 7 per cent per annum. With concessional aid flows declining in real terms and with new aid criteria being based more on self-interest than on a genuine concern for the problems of the poor, the basic needs requirement is almost certainly destined to remain unachieved.

With respect to the multilateral sources of finance, the amounts available, while useful, remain small. IDA, the World Bank's soft-loan affiliate, has been disbursing on average no more than $1.4 billion per annum between 1976 and 1981 in spite of rising loan commitments.[6] The Trust Fund of the IMF,[7] in the three years of its operations, 1978 to 1980 distributed SDRs 827 million to eligible countries, and loans available on concessional terms to poor countries facing balance of payments problems totalled SDRs 3 billion in the period 1977 to 1981.

Dissatisfaction with current institutional arrangements and the dismal prospects for the transfer of resources to the developing countries in general, and the least-developed in particular, have led to several proposals being put forward with the aim of boosting the flow. The oldest and most well-known of these is the proposal that reserve creation by the IMF should be linked to

the provision of development finance: the SDR-Aid-Link.
Having its origins in Keynes' proposal at Bretton Woods in
1944 for the creation of an International Clearing Union,
it was elaborated in the "Stamp Plan" of 1962. This plan
envisaged an enlarged IMF distributing to the LDCs certificates of deposit for use in purchasing imports from the
developed countries; these latter countries would accept
the certificates and hold them as part of their international reserves.[8] A similar proposal has been advanced
by Scitovsky.[9] As the proposal now stands, newly-created
SDRs would be allocated not on the basis of existing IMF
Quotas but disproportionately in favour of the developing
countries; by so doing both the needs of international
liquidity and of development finance would be met.
Numerous arguments for and against the link have been
advanced in several quarters,[10] but the failure of the
proposal to be implemented in any form is perhaps the
result of four fundamental misgivings on the part of the
IMF itself and of the developed countries:

1. The concern that since the sum of liquidity
   and development needs is so great, the creation of SDRs sufficient to meet those needs
   will be inflationary for the world economy
   as a whole.

2. As a result of the larger amount in circula-
   tion, the attractiveness of the SDR as a
   reserve asset would be reduced in the eyes
   of developed-country reserve holders.

3. Concern, especially in the United States,
   that increased LDC demand for SDRs would
   reduce the demand for the dollar, leading to
   its further weakness; and

4. Perhaps, most importantly, the general
   unwillingness in the developed countries to
   concede to an automatic mechanism for
   channelling funds to developing countries.

This feeling derives firstly from the
widespread opinion, strengthened by experience, that LDC economic management systems
are not as efficient as they should be in
utilizing scarce foreign exchange, and
secondly that political influence gained
in the developing countries would be
reduced as the importance of bilateral aid
declines in favour of the new mechanism.

With the current emphasis in international monetary
affairs on combating inflation, strengthening the dollar
and other national currencies, on promoting the SDR as a
widely acceptable reserve asset, and on the need for
adjustment in the LDCs as against mere financing of
deficits, the prospects for implementation of the proposal
appear dim indeed.

Of the other proposals for increasing the flow of
external finance to the developing countries,[11] the most
prominent has been that put forward by Michalopoulos.[12]
He suggests that substantial additional flows of external
finance would be available to the LDCs if the developed
countries, and institutions such as the OECD and OPEC,
were to guarantee borrowing by the developing countries
from the private capital markets and the multilateral
financial institutions.

This proposal has gained support from, among others,
one of Japan's major financial institutions, the Sumitomo
Bank. It has proposed the establishment of a new institution that would operate the guarantee scheme. Borrowers
would pay a fee of 0.5 per cent for securing the guarantee
which would cover interest payments in the event of
default. The guarantee fund would be financed from contributions by the IMF and by revenues obtained from borrowers' fees.[13]

The guarantee scheme has also been supported by the
President of the IDB, who has stated:

> ...I believe it essential to adopt immedi-
> ately the measures needed to establish sys-
> tems of guarantees granted by the developed
> countries to the multinational lending agen-
> cies. In this way, these agencies can
> mobilize the additional capital resources in
> the international markets in amounts suffi-
> cient to meet the urgent external financing
> requirements of the developing countries,
> thereby allowing them to continue to grow at
> the rates they achieved on their own before
> the current crisis.[14]

The reasoning behind the proposal is that investors
are primarily concerned with risk aversion. By having
LDC borrowing guaranteed by the rich countries, risk is
minimized and repayment is assured. Guarantees have been
used for centuries in banking but normally as a secondary
form of support and not as the primary consideration,
which is usually that the borrower has the capacity to
repay the loan out of his own earnings. Consequently, the
use of guarantees as the only inducement to otherwise
unwilling lenders and in the absence of which the borrowing country could not hope to market its bonds or obtain
its loan, is not likely to be met with much enthusiasm by
prospective lenders.[15]

In spite of funding difficulties until recently faced
by the World Bank, and which continue to be experienced by
the regional development banks, proposals continue to be
put forward recommending the creation of new institutions
to channel resources to the developing countries. Bird,
for example, has suggested the creation of a new development institution whose functions would be to grant
general-purpose aid and loans to meet debt-servicing
obligations of the least-developed countries.[16] Funded
by contributions from the rich countries or by the creation of SDRs, the institution would also provide guarantees to enable developing countries to gain access to the
private financial markets. Proposals for such an institution have also been put forward by the "Group of 24",

representing the views of the LDCs in the IMF,[17] by
UNCTAD, and by the Brandt Commission.

Finally, proposals have been put forward for
increasing the supply of external finance to the LDCs by
taxes on the "brain-drain" from the developing countries
and on the mining of the sea bed. The "brain-drain" proposal, first advanced by Bhagwati,[18] envisages a tax on
qualified and professional people emigrating to the
developed countries. Revenues may be collected by the
tax authorities in the developed countries and remitted to
the relevant developing countries. Estimated revenues
from this source total around $500 million per annum.
However, because of the many political, moral, and admin-
istrative arguments against the proposal its implementation is not regarded as feasible in the near future.[19]

Taxes on ocean resources for redistribution to poor
countries were estimated by Cooper to be capable of yielding about $5 billion per annum by the end of the present
century.[20] However, as pointed out by Cline,[21] the
initial potential of this source has been much reduced by
the agreement at the Third U.N. Law of the Sea Conference,
to sanction individual countries' sovreignty over a
200-mile economic zone extending from their shores.

One proposal that is supported by a few academic
writers but which is rarely mentioned in official circles
is that concessional aid should now be redistributed away
from the higher income developing countries to the low
income group. As Cline remarks:

> ... it is important to retain the principle of
> "aid graduation," as individual developing
> countries reach higher per capita income levels,
> they should "graduate" from concessional aid to
> resource flows on market-related terms from
> both official and private sources.[22]

While the proposal has been given much lip-service by
aid-donors, its full implementation at the bilateral level
will not be possible as long as aid-giving criteria

include such factors as the political, strategic, and
trading importance of the recipient, rather than a concern for basic needs. OECD data for 1980 show that
higher-income countries and oil-producers received concessional assistance totalling almost $1 billion, while
the least-developed countries received $5.5 billion; as
a percentage of GNP, OECD net bilateral aid to low-income
countries was only 0.09 in 1980.[23] While these countries
have ready access to commercial and World Bank funds, the
poorest countries have no such flexibility of sources and
need to rely almost exclusively on concessional assistance. The time is, therefore, long overdue for the
OECD to devote a larger share of concessional assistance
to the least developed countries than the existing 50 per
cent. In this context, it is encouraging to note that the
World Bank has agreed in principle to begin phasing
higher-income LDCs (with per capita incomes in 1980
dollars over $2650) out of its concessional lending pro-
grammes.

In this effort, the high-income developing countries
also have an important role to play. In the past they
have not hesitated to join in attacks against the industrial countries for creating and perpetuating inequali-
ties in the distribution of world resources. By giving
their support to the "aid graduation" principle they
would be making a vital contribution to the reduction of
inequality while, at the same time helping the people of
the least-developed countries in their struggle against
poverty.

Finally, in an extension of this proposal,
Diaz-Alejandro has suggested that the World Bank should
discriminate in favour of the poorer countries with
respect to lending charges:

> "Indeed, the rationale justifying Brazilian,
> Nigerian, and Philippine borrowing from the
> IBRD (excluding IDA credits) at terms simi-
> lar to those of Haiti, Ethiopia and Bangladesh

is far from self-evident and persuasive. As
LDC heterogeneity becomes more marked the
traditional multilateral intermediaries would
do well to concentrate their attention on the
least developed countries, raising the price
at which their services, including technical
help, are made available to the more fortunate
LDCs."[24]

In conclusion, while the international banking system
has undertaken the bulk of the burden of providing the
external financing needed for sustained growth in the
middle-and high-income developing countries, the traditional, bilateral aid donors have failed to respond
similarly to the needs of those countries which are in
greatest need of concessional assistance. Proposals for
increasing the flow of funds remain mere proposals and
prospects for the future of the least-developed nations
appear gloomy. A major effort of political will is therefore needed on the part of all other countries if the
problem of poverty is to be overcome in the near future.
Unfortunately, it is precisely political will, and
genuine concern for the welfare of the poor that seem to
be in short supply at this time.

11
Conclusion

It would not be an exaggeration to conclude that external finance provided by the international banking system has facilitated the achievement of quite satisfactory rates of economic growth in several non-oil developing countries at a time when the recession in industrial countries and inadequate flows of external assistance from the traditional aid donors and the multilateral agencies have been combining ominously to threaten the economic well-being of the LDC group of countries. The banks have been able to achieve this by their efficiency in extending onto the international arena their traditional domestic banking function of transferring savings into investment.

The eurocurrency markets have been the medium through which billions of dollars have been transferred from the vast pool of international savings[1] to the LDCs, and in spite of the severe shocks to which the banking system has been subject in the past decade, the soundness of the markets has remained relatively unaffected. However, largely because of prudential considerations, the banks cannot, for very long, continue to lend at the pace at which they have in the past. The low spreads charged to prime borrowers have given rise to concern about the adequacy of the banks' capital base. U.S. money-centre banks have experienced a fall in the

ratio of equity capital to total assets from 4.5 per cent
at the end of 1972 to 3.5 per cent at the end of September
1979 and this trend has continued.[2] In addition, some
major countries may be approaching prudential limits set
by the banks on individual borrowers. However, in seeking to diversify their portfolios, the banks will be
looking to increase the rate at which they lend to
smaller, creditworthy borrowers, although at higher
spreads than obtain at present. Even for the major banks
with large individual country exposures, therefore, there
is room for expansion of lending in the medium-term. In
addition to general purpose country lending, the major
banks are likely to become more involved in project
finance, trade finance, and co-financings. Quite apart
from the largest banks, smaller, regional U.S., European,
Japanese and Arab banks have recently been increasing
their portfolio of lending in non-oil LDCs. Arab banks,
for example, have increased their share of total LDC
lending from 8 per cent in 1979 to 32 per cent in 1980.[3]
Prospects for the medium-term, therefore, point to a continued, though modest, rate of growth of bank lending to
the developing countries. Indeed, the recent Group of
Thirty document on the Outlook for International Banking
reported that banks expect to continue to see lending to
LDCs grow as a proportion of total lending.[4] The demand
for external finance seems certain to continue, given the
pessimistic balance of payments forecasts for the medium
term. With respect to supply, in the context of an
increasing number of reschedulings, and pressure on
international earnings, banks are likely to become more
selective, and more cautious and rigorous in their
country analysis. Policy-makers in prospective borrowing
countries will need to demonstrate much more clearly, the
ability to manage their economies efficiently.
    As a result of these considerations, and in the
interests of the stability of the international financial

system, the time has come for non-bank sources of finance
to bear a larger share of the task of providing foreign-
currency to the non-oil LDCs. Until recently, while there
has been much rhetoric on the part of these sources
expressing concern with the growing financial needs of the
LDCs, not much concrete action has been forthcoming. The
doubling of the World Bank's capital and the introduction
of new or liberalized facilities within the IMF have been
welcome developments, but bolder actions are required.

In the IMF, the process of facilitating easier access
to its resources needs to be accelerated with special
emphasis being placed on reducing the required speed of
adjustment. The influence of the institution within the
international monetary system might be greatly enhanced if
funds available to individual countries were greater than
they are at present. In this context, it is most
encouraging to note that the Managing-Director of the
Fund, has, in a recent speech, stated that in view of the
large deficits being faced by countries:

> ... the Fund must, if necessary, be prepared
> to engage directly in re-cycling activities
> proper, i.e. borrow funds from countries in
> a position to lend them.[5]

A stronger, more dynamic IMF is essential if the institution is to play its part in the transfer of resources to
the LDCs.

Regional development banks which have contributed
much to the development of the poorer countries of Africa,
Asia, and the Caribbean can assist further by working to
increase their capital and by continuing in their efforts
to tap national and international capital markets for
long-term funds.

In the absence of any marked increase in the volume
of concessional aid in the near future, there is need for
statesmanship and much political will in both the
developed countries and the richer LDCs if such assistance
is to be channelled primarily to those areas in greatest

need: the least-developed countries. There is also the
need for OPEC to play a more direct role in lending part
of its large surplus to the non-oil developing countries.
This may be achieved by:

1. Lending directly to the richer LDCs through
   bond issues or central bank to central bank
   loans.
2. Lending to the multilateral financial institutions and the regional development banks
   for on-lending to individual countries, and
3. Increasing the flow of concessional aid to
   non-Islamic countries which have been seriously affected by the oil price increases.

Since OPEC price increases have been a major source
of balance of payments problems in the non-oil countries,
and since OPEC professes solidarity with the LDCs, the
organization should perhaps be increasing its efforts to
assist in financing the deficits. At this time, attention
needs to be focussed beyond the narrow North-South discussions to a broader framework with OPEC sharing a
larger proportion of the burden than it presently does.
It is unfortunate that attempts to introduce OPEC into the
discussions at UNCTAD and elsewhere have not been very
successful.

Especially in the case of large projects, co-finan-
ing by two or more lenders appears to offer the best
opportunity for an optimum mix of sources of finance to
the LDCs. Several projects have already been financed in
this way with the World Bank and the IDB acting as loan
co-ordinators.[6] An excellent example of the possibilities available was the financing of the expansion programme of a major Brazilian steel company (CSN). The
World Bank provided $95 million, IDB's contribution was
$63 million, private commercial banks provided a medium-
term eurocurrency loan of $55 million, and export credits
contributed $490 million.[7] In the year-ending June 1981,

co-financing arranged by the IBRD totalled $4 billion, of
which $1.7 billion was supplied by banks. The possibili-
ties for co-financing, involving the banks, the IMF, OPEC,
and the development finance institutions, are exciting and
could well be the best means available of increasing the
flow of funds to the LDCs.

International banks will continue to contribute to
the growth process in non-oil developing countries in
general, and well-managed LDCs in particular, for some
time. However, action along the lines briefly discussed
above will be required of other agencies in order to
reduce the present burden on the banks and to ensure the
continued stability of the international financial system
on which the prosperity of the world economy depends.

Appendix

Countries are classified along the lines used by the World Bank in their World Development Report 1979:

(i) Developing Countries:
are divided into the following income groups based on 1977 GNP per capita:

Low Income: with per capita of US$300 and below

Middle Income: with per capita of above US$300.

(ii) Capital Surplus
Oil Exporters: Kuwait, Libya, Oman, Quatar, Saudi Arabia, UAE other major oil producers are grouped among Developing Countries.

(iii) Industrialized Countries: Members of OECD except Greece, Portugal, Spain, and Turkey, which are grouped with the Middle Income Developing Countries.

(iv) Centrally Planned Countries: Albania, Bulgaria, China, Cuba, Czechoslovakia, The German Democratic Republic, Hungary, North Korea, Mongolia, Poland, Romania, the USSR.

    (v) <u>OECD</u>: Australia, Austria, Belgium, Canada,
Denmark, Finland, France, Germany, Greece,
Iceland, Italy, Japan, Luxembourg, Nether-
lands, New Zealand, Norway, Portugal,
Spain, Sweden, Switzerland, Turkey, U.K.,
U.S.A.

It is recognized that the developing countries are
not a homogenous group of countries with common physical
features, economic structures, and levels of income. The
usual sub-divisions: low-income, and middle-income
countries, while highlighting the special characteristics
and problems of the poorest countries, encourage the
notion that all other countries can conveniently be classified and analyzed as a group. This practice (in common
with many generalizations in the social sciences) tends to
lead to sweeping statements and inappropriate policy-pre-
scriptions which may damage the growth prospects of an
already poor country.

To some extent, this book also succumbs to this tendency. It is hoped that in spite of the generalizations,
the essential aspects of the book prove to be of some
relevance to individual countries.

Perhaps the time has now come to re-classify what are
now termed "developing countries" into more meaningful
sub-groups. Already the OECD uses the term "Newly
Industrialising Countries" (NICS) to describe those
developing countries which

> ... are characterised by a fast growth of the
> level and share of industrial employment, an
> enlargement of export market shares in manu-
> factures and a rapid relative reduction in the
> real per capita income gap separating them
> from the advanced industrial countries.[1]

---

1) OECD: "The Impact of the Newly Industrialising
Countries on Production and Trade in Manufactures."
OECD, Paris 1979, p. 6.

The countries are: Brazil, Greece, Hong-Kong, Korea,
Mexico, Portugal, Singapore, Spain, Taiwan and
Yugoslavia.

TABLE 1

NON-OIL DEVELOPING COUNTRIES: CURRENT ACCOUNT FINANCING, 1973-81

(In billions of U.S. dollars)

	1973	1974	1975	1976	1977	1978	1979	1980	1981
Current account deficit[1]	11.6	37.0	46.5	32.0	28.3	39.2	58.9	86.2	99.0
Financing through transactions that do not affect net debt positions, of which,	10.1	13.0	11.8	12.0	14.9	17.2	23.0	24.1	26.3
Net unrequited transfers received by governments of non-oil developing countries	5.4	6.9	7.1	7.4	8.3	8.2	10.9	12.3	12.9
Direct investment flows, net	4.3	5.3	5.3	4.7	5.3	6.9	9.2	10.0	13.6
Net borrowing and use of reserves	1.5	23.9	34.7	20.1	13.4	22.0	35.9	62.1	72.7
Reduction of reserve assets (accumulation -)	-9.7	-2.4	1.9	-13.8	-12.4	-15.8	-12.4	-4.9	-1.6
Net external borrowing, of which,	11.2	23.3	32.9	31.2	25.8	37.8	48.4	67.1	74.3
Long-term borrowing	11.7	19.5	26.6	27.9	26.5	35.3	37.9	45.5	55.8
From official sources	5.4	9.3	11.4	10.8	12.6	14.2	15.4	20.5	20.2
From financial institutions	7.1	12.6	13.8	17.0	19.4	23.9	32.4	30.1	35.5
Use of reserve-related credit facilities[2]	0.2	1.7	2.5	4.4	-0.1	0.5	-0.6	1.7	5.4
Other short-term borrowing, net	0.2	5.2	6.4	12.2	0.8	4.7	-10.5)	19.9	13.1
Residual errors and omissions	-0.8	-	-2.7	-11.2	-1.1	-2.5	0.5)		

1) Net total of balances on goods, services, and private transfers.
2) Comprises use of Fund credit and short-term borrowing by monetary authorities from other monetary authorities.

SOURCE: IMF Annual Report 1982

TABLE 2

CHANGES IN THE TERMS OF TRADE[1]

(Percentage changes)

	Average 1963-72	Change from Preceding Year								
		1973	1974	1975	1976	1977	1978	1979	1980	1981
Industrial countries	0.3	-1.6	-11.9	2.7	-1.0	-1.1	2.7	-2.6	-7.6	-0.6
Oil exporting countries	0.5	11.8	138.4	-5.4	5.8	0.6	-10.7	28.6	41.6	11.5
Non-oil developing countries	-	6.1	- 5.6	-9.0	6.0	6.0	- 4.1	-0.3	-4.3	-2.2
Reference:										
Percentage Changes in World Trade										
Prices for Major Commodity Groups										
(a) Manufactures	3.0	17.7	21.8	12.3	-	9.0	14.7	14.5	11.0	-5.0
(b) Oil	3.0	40.0	225.8	5.1	6.3	9.3	0.1	48.7	61.9	10.1
(c) Non-oil primary commodity (market prices)	2.5	53.2	28.0	-18.2	13.3	20.7	-4.7	16.5	9.7	-14.8

1) Based on Foreign Trade Unit Values

SOURCE: IMF Annual Report 1982.

TABLE 3

IBRD/IDA LOANS 1970-1981

(US$ millions)

							Fiscal Year					
	1970	1971	1972	1973	1974	1975	1976	1977	1978	1979	1980	1981
WORLD BANK												
Loans	1580	1921	1966	2051	3218	4320	4977	5759	6098	6989	7644	8809
Disbursements	754	915	1182	1180	1533	1995	2470	2636	2787	3602	4363	5063
NUMBERS												
Operations Approved	69	78	72	73	105	122	141	161	137	142	144	140
Countries	39	42	40	42	49	51	51	54	46	44	48	50
IDA												
Credit Amounts	606	584	1000	1357	1095	1576	1655	1308	2313	3022	3838	3482
Disbursements	143	235	261	493	711	1026	1252	1298	1062	1222	1411	1878
NUMBERS												
Operations Approved	50	51	68	75	69	68	73	67	99	105	103	106
Countries	33	34	38	43	41	39	39	36	42	43	40	40
TOTAL												
Loans	2186	2505	2966	3408	4313	4896	6632	7067	8411	10011	11482	12291
Disbursements	897	1150	1443	1673	2244	3021	3722	3934	3849	4824	5774	6941

SOURCE: World Bank: Annual Report 1981

TABLE 4

NET AMOUNTS OUTSTANDING TO INTERNATIONAL COMMERCIAL BANKS

BY SELECTED NON-OIL DEVELOPING COUNTRIES, AS AT END

DECEMBER 1981

(US$ millions)

The Caribbean and South America

Cuba	1312
Dominican Republic	303
Jamaica	298
Argentina	16345
Brazil	44917
Chile	5981
Costa Rica	532
El Salvador	40
Guyana	71
Nicaragua	419

Africa

Cameroon	560
Chad	3
Congo	341
Ivory Coast	2077
Liberia	4551
Malawi	98
Morocco	2635
Niger	326
Senegal	224
Sudan	134
Tanzania	71
Togo	124
Tunisia	131
Zaire	228
Zambia	148

Asia

Burma	66
Hong Kong	5515
North Korea	315
South Korea	13786
New Hebrides	-
Philippines	4278
Thailand	1737
Vietnam	245

SOURCE: BIS.

TABLE 5

NON-OIL DEVELOPING COUNTRIES: LONG-TERM EXTERNAL DEBT, 1973-81

(In billions of U.S. dollars)

	1973	1974	1975	1976	1977	1978	1979	1980	1981
Total outstanding debt of non-oil developing countries	96.8	120.1	146.8	181.4	221.8	276.4	324.4	375.4	436.9
By type of creditor									
Official creditors	48.3	58.2	67.9	82.2	98.2	117.4	133.3	155.5	175.6
Governments	35.7	42.6	48.5	57.5	67.4	79.6	88.9	102.1	114.3
International institutions	12.6	15.7	19.4	24.7	30.8	37.8	44.5	53.4	61.4
Private creditors	48.5	61.8	78.9	99.2	123.6	159.0	191.1	220.0	261.4
Unguaranteed debt	20.6	25.3	31.5	38.7	44.0	52.4	58.6	68.8	84.8
Guaranteed debt	27.9	36.5	47.4	60.5	79.6	106.6	132.5	151.2	176.5
Financial institutions	14.0	22.8	31.2	41.9	57.5	75.4	101.9	117.4	138.8
Other private creditors	13.9	13.8	16.2	18.6	22.1	31.2	30.6	33.8	37.7
By area									
Africa	13.1	15.9	19.9	24.2	31.7	38.7	44.7	49.2	56.0
Asia	27.0	31.5	36.7	43.9	53.0	62.9	71.6	85.6	102.8
Europe	11.6	14.0	16.2	20.8	25.4	33.5	44.0	54.2	60.2
Middle East	8.5	10.1	13.1	16.0	20.3	24.6	28.3	32.9	36.7
Western Hemisphere	36.6	48.5	60.9	76.5	91.4	116.7	135.8	153.4	181.2

SOURCE: IMF Annual Report, 1982.

Notes

CHAPTER 1
(1)   World Bank, (166).
(2)   Johnson (82)   293.

CHAPTER 2
(1)   See R.F. Harrod; "An Essay in Dynamic Theory,"
      Economic Journal, Vol. 49, 1939, 14-33, and
      Towards a Dynamic Economics, (Macmillan, London,
      1948) and E.D. Domar; Essays in the Theory of
      Economic Growth, (Oxford University Press, New
      York, 1957).
(2)   For a critical analysis of the use of models in
      economic development and especially of the use of
      the "capital/output ratio" concept, see Streeten
      (156) Chapters 5 and 6.
(3)   Reynolds (142)   312.
(4)   See R. Solow; "A Contribution to the Theory of
      Economic Growth," Quarterly Journal of Economics,
      February, 1956, 65-94.
(5)   See J. Meade; A Neo-Classical Theory of Economic
      Growth (Unwin, London, 1962).
(6)   See Lewis (98) and Lipton (105).
(7)   Mikesell   (121).

(8)   Hahn and Matthews, (72) 890.

(9)   Mikesell op. cit. 32.

(10) Sen (152) 33.

(11) The Manchester School, Vol. 22, No. 2, 1954.

(12) See Leeson (95) 199.

(13) Lewis (104).

(14) As now occurs on an international basis in the case
      of Egyptian and Turkish migrant labour in the
      Middle East and Western Europe.

(15) T.W. Schultz; Transforming Traditional Agricul-
      ture. (Yale University Press, New Haven, 1964), 5.

(16) Lewis (104), 217.

(17) See, for example applications of his basic frame-
      work by Ahluwalia et al (2), Lipton (105), Kelly
      et al (88), and Galbis (62).

(18) See Bhagwati (ed.) (15), and Cline (ed.) (35) for
      excellent analyses of the issues in these dis-
      cussions.

(19) Shaw (153), McKinnon (113), (114), Galbis (62).

(20) Schumpeter (151) 85.

(21) American Economic Review, Vol. 45, September 1955,
      515-516.

(22) See also Spellman (154) and Kelly et al (88) on
      this theme.

(23) McKinnon (113) Chapter 8.

(24) Galbis, (62).

(25) The possible incompatibility between creditworthi-
      ness and national-income growth is recognized by
      Galbis, op. cit., 69-70.

(26) Bhatia and Khatkhate (18) 152.

(27) IBRD Annual Report 1981.

(28) Kindleberger (91), 136.

(29) Meier (118), 62.

(30) Ibid., 62.

(31) Friedman (60).

(32)   McKinnon (112).

(33)   Chenery and Strout (31).

(34)   Michalopoulos (119) 289.

(35)   While the link no doubt exists, it does not
       necessarily imply causality between capital flows
       and growth. See Cairncross (27) and Pazos (138).

(36)   Machlup (109) 5.

(37)   Johnson (80) 53.

CHAPTER 3

(1)   For a fuller account of this see Einzig (53).

(2)   A complete history of the Medici Bank is available
       in Kirshner (92) and De Roover (44).

(3)   Davis (43) 10.

(4)   Sayers (150) 1.

(5)   Cameron (29) 54-55.

(6)   Much of this account of Belgian banking derives
       from Cameron op. cit., 144 et seq.

(7)   Ibid., 145

(8)   Gerschenkron (63) 14-16.

(9)   Patrick (137).

(10)   Yamamura (167).

(11)   Sayers (150) 186-188.

(12)   For an interesting account of country lending by
       banks from 1817 to the present see Morgan and
       Thomas (123).

(13)   Data from Aldcroft (4), Chapter 10, and Lewis (101),
       177.

(14)   Berrill (11) 295-297. For the role of external bor-
       rowing in the early development of Australia and
       Sweden see Myrdal (128) 98-99.

(15)   Hagen (71) 352.

(16)   Horvat (77) 235.

(17)   Thomas (159) 10.

(18)   Aldcroft (4) 240.

CHAPTER 4

(1) See, for example E.J. Mishan; The Costs of Economic
     Growth, (Staples Press, London, 1967), and
     D. Meadows et al; The Limits of Growth. (Universe
     Books, New York, 1972).

(2) Bhagwati (14) 35. The "overriding priority" of
     rapid growth is also stressed in the Brandt Com-
     mission Report (21), 129.

(3) Beckerman (9) 9.

(4) Ortiz-Mena (135), 15-16.

(5) World Bank, World Development Report, 1981.

(6) See the Foreword to Cline (ed.) (35) by Sewell and
     Kallab.

(7) On the growing interdependence between developing
     and developed countries see Brandt (21) Chapter 3.

(8) Sources: IBRD (166), 277, and IMF: International
     Financial Statistics (IFS) Yearbook 1979.

(9) IMF: World Economic Outlook. April 1982.

(10) Ibid.

(11) The 6-Month Libor rate moved from an average of 9
     per cent in 1978 to over 16 per cent in 1981.

(12) IMF: World Economic Outlook. 1982.

(13) For a proposal to extend currency convertibility to
     the LDCs see McKinnon (115) 270-291.

(14) Data from World Bank: World Development Report 1979,
     134-135.

CHAPTER 5

(1) IMF: World Economic Outlook. 1982.

(2) World Bank 1979 Report, 142-143.

(3) For example, Brazil, Costa Rica, Hong Kong, The
     Philippines, Singapore, South Korea, Taiwan, and
     Yugoslavia.

(4) For a discussion of the trade and growth prospects
     of this group of countries see, OECD (132).

(5) IMF: International Financial Statistics (IFS)
     Yearbook 1979, 63.

138

(6)   Associations of banana, iron ore, mercury, and oil
      seed producers now exist in addition to the older-
      established sugar, coffee, and cocoa associations.

(7)   See Marian Radetzki; "The Potential for Monopolis-
      tic Commodity Pricing by Developing Countries," and
      Paul Streeten: "The Dynamics of the New Poor
      Power," both in G.K. Helleiner (ed.) 1976, at 53
      and 77 respectively.

(8)   See Appendix Table 2.

(9)   IMF Survey, April 19, 1982.

(10) IMF: World Economic Outlook. 1982.

(11) See McNamara (116) on the costs of increasing pro-
      tectionism.

(12) Lewis (102) and (103).

(13) Ohlin (134) 219.

(14) Development Assistance refers to aid on conces-
      sional terms.

(15) OECD, (133).

(16) OECD: "Development Co-operation." 1978 Review. 19.

(17) Financial Times, 22nd November, 1979.

(18) The Banker, November 1979, 46.

(19) Financial Times, 29th January, 1980.

(20) For a brief discussion of these constraints see
      OECD (133).

(21) (108). 6.

(22) The Economist, 23rd February, 1980. 67.

(23) OECD, op. cit. 85.

(24) IMF: World Economic Outlook 1982. 45.

(25) IFS Yearbooks 1979 and 1981.

(26) For details of this loan, see IMF Survey. 9th
      November, 1981.

(27) Access to this facility is open to members in need
      of funds larger than that available under normal
      credit facilities.
      For a more detailed discussion of the new measures
      see IMF Survey 21st May, 1979.

(28) IMF Survey, 4th February 1980, and IFS. July, 1982.

(29) Fiscal years. See Appendix Table 3.

(30) Total borrowing in fiscal 1981 amounted to $5069 million. World Bank Annual Report 1981, 11.

(31) IMF Survey, 15th October, 1979.

(32) IMF: World Economic Outlook. 1982.

(33) See Franko (59), 129. It is estimated that about 80 per cent of all foreign investment in the manufacturing sector in Latin America is concentrated in Argentina, Brazil, Mexico, and Venezuela.

(34) Amex Bank Review, 28th January, 1980.

(35) For an account of Ghana's difficulties arising out of large borrowings on export credits see Krassowski, (93), Bitterman, (20) 167-173, and Grayson (65).

(36) For a useful introduction to the bond markets see Einzig, The Eurobond Market. (Macmillan, London 1969).

(37) IMF Survey, 3rd September 1979, 273-282.

(38) European Investment Bank: Annual Report. 1981.

(39) See Appendix II. Table 1.

CHAPTER 6

(1) IMF: World Economic Outlook. 1982, 166.

(2) For the reasons for this see IBRD: Borrowing in International Capital Markets, Second Quarter 1979.

(3) Sources IMF, BIS.

(4) BIS.

(5) See Crockett and Knight (40), Sargen (148), Fishlow (57), and Table 5.2.

(6) For some details see Sargen (149), Feder and Just (56), Dizard (49), Friedman (61), Kapur (87), and Nagy (130).

(7)   IMF Survey. 19th July, 1982. 211.

(8)   See IMF: World Economic Outlook 1982. IBRD: World
       Development Report, 1981, and various issues of
       Morgan Guaranty: World Financial Markets, and Amex
       Bank Review.

CHAPTER 7

(1)   See, for example, Fishlow (57) and Ruding (146).

(2)   Kindleberger (91) and Meier (118).

(3)   Diaz-Alejandro (46), 190.

(4)   Lewis (102), 65.

(5)   Wellons, (163).

(6)   See Friedman (60), Hang-Shen Cheng (74), Nagy (131),
       and Sargen (148).

(7)   Diaz-Alejandro. (46) 192-193.

(8)   IFS: Supplement on Fund Accounts. 1982.

(9)   IMF Survey, 21st May, 1979.

(10)   IMF Annual Report 1978, 48.

(11)   Fishlow (57) 136.

(12)   See Wellons (163) 45 for examples of this policy in
       Brazil, Colombia, the Ivory Coast and the Philip-
       pines.

(13)   For a discussion on the utility of an adequate level
       of international liquidity in a developing country
       see Kindleberger (91).

(14)   Little et al. (106), 155. See also Bhagwati and
       Desai (12), 198-214.

(15)   Little et al., op. cit., 56.

(16)   Ul Haq. (160) 327.

(17)   Ibid. 331.

(18)   Tendler (158) 75-80.

(19)   Streeten (156), 7.

(20)   For a cautious view of this strategy see the dis-
       cussion: "The Drive to Refinance in the Euromar-
       kets." Euromoney, October 1978.

(21)   Pazos (138).

CHAPTER 8
(1)   Joshi (86) 262.
(2)   William Gaud, then head of the International
      Finance Corporation, in a speech on 7th November
      1973. Quoted from Diaz-Alejandro (46) 191-192.
(3)   Financial Times, 31st May 1979, 13.
(4)   Rockefeller (145).
(5)   The United States, Canada, Japan, Belgium, Sweden,
      France, Germany, Italy, the Netherlands, the United
      Kingdom.
(6)   For a discussion on this see World Financial
      Markets, March 1979.
(7)   See IMF: Annual Reports, various issues, and
      Ruding (146).
(8)   A view shared by Caldwell and Villamill in the case
      of Zaire. (28). See also Wellons (163) 124-127.
(9)   Wellons, op. cit., 117-130.
(10) Indeed, it is because spreads on lending to LDCs
      have been so low until recently that fears were
      being expressed that sufficient earnings were not
      being made on international lending to maintain the
      capital adequacy of the banks.
(11) Friedman (60), 39.
(12) Algeria, Argentina, Brazil, Indonesia, Mexico,
      Spain, and Yugoslavia.
(13) World Bank: World Development 1979, 30-31.
(14) Amex Bank Review. Vol. 8. 1981. No. 8/9.
(15) Argentina, Brazil, Chile, Mexico, Peru, and
      Venezuela.
(16) Amex Bank Review, Vol. 6, 1979. No. 12.
(17) BIS.
(18) Financial Times 13th December 1979. See also the
      issue of 31st December 1979.
(19) See BIS Annual Reports 1979 to 1981.
(20) Burns (25), 461.

(21)   Speech at the annual banquet of the Overseas
       Bankers Club, London, February 1979. Reported in
       The Banker, March 1979.

(22)   Morse (124), 142.

CHAPTER 9

(1)   Myint (127), 17.

(2)   See Leith (97) for the presence of this notion in
       Ghana under Nkrumah. See also Myrdal (128), 222-224.

(3)   See for example Cairncross (27), Bauer (8), and
       Friedman (60).

(4)   Osvaldo Sunkel: "Underdevelopment in Latin America:
       Toward the Year 2000" in Bhagwati (ed.): Economics
       and World Order - From the 1970s to the 1990s.
       (Macmillan, New York, 1972), 220.

(5)   Mikesell (121), 258.

(6)   Bhagwati and Desai (12).

(7)   Brimmer (22).

(8)   Helleiner (ed.), 1976, 16-17.

(9)   As noted by Kindleberger (89).

(10)   (108), 3-4.

(11)   Wellons (163) notes that eurocurrency loans have
       been used to finance airlines and airport con-
       struction, army-officer housing, and other govern-
       ment buildings in Zaire.

(12)   Green (66), 267.

(13)   For example Brazil and the Philippines.

(14)   Financial Times, 18th March 1980.

(15)   Islam (79), 231-232.

(16)   This results from the well-known "J-Curve" effect
       of a devaluation in its early stages.

(17)   See Amex Bank Review, Vol. 6, No. 11.

(18)   For a list of these studies see Bhagwati and
       Srinivasan (17).

(19)   (106), 324.

(20)   (17). 15-16.

(21)   Ortiz-Mena (135), 143.

(22)   IMF Annual Report 1979, 40-44.   See also Krueger
       (94).

(23)   See for example Little et al (106), Leith (97),
       Diaz-Alejandro (47), and Bhagwati and Desai (12).

(24)   Leith (97), 96.

(25)   Lipton (105), 321-323.

(26)   Ibib.   This amount was equivalent to 29 per cent of
       total agricultural incomes.

(27)   Weisskopf (162), 59.

(28)   As noted by Little et al (106), 208-211.

(29)   See Little et al, op. cit., 5 and 213, and
       Bhagwati and Desai (12), 324-325.

(30)   As observed by Leith in Ghana (97), 104-105.

(31)   Goldsmith (64), Shaw (153), McKinnon (113).

(32)   For data on interest rates prevailing in LDCs see
       IFS Yearbook 1981.

(33)   See Bhagwati (14) 113, and Please (140), 160-161.

(34)   Lipton (105), 246-247.

(35)   On the importance of rural savings see D.W. Adams:
       "Mobilizing Household Savings through Rural Finan-
       cial Markets." Economic Development and Cultural
       Change, Vol. 26, 547-560.

(36)   A. Basch: Financing Economic Development.
       (Macmillan, New York 1964) 85-86.   Quoted from
       Perera (139) Chapter 5.

(37)   World Bank.   World Development Report, 1979, 108.

(38)   Friedman (60) 25.

(39)   Caldwell and Villamil (28), 135.

(40)   p. 32.

(41)   Myint (126) 33-36.

(42)   Friedman, op. cit., 29.

(43)   For a fuller account of possible policy measures
       appropriate to LDCs see Bela Belassa: Policy Reform
       in Developing Countries, (Pergamon Press, New York)
       1977.

CHAPTER 10

(1) See Appendix I, for definition of country groupings.

(2) OECD: Development Co-operation Review. 1981. 60.

(3) For an elaboration of these basic needs see Streeten and Burki (157). Other useful references are Ahluwalia et al (2), and Brandt (21). Chapters 4 and 5.

(4) See Cline (35) for the various estimates, 336-338.

(5) OECD, (133).

(6) See IBRD Annual Report 1981.

(7) The Trust Fund was financed from profits arising from gold sales by the IMF.

(8) See Meier (118), 304.

(9) T. Scitovsky: "Requirements of an International Reserve System." International Finance Section. Princeton University, November 1965.

(10) For useful discussions of the proposal see Cline (34), Haan (70), Meier (118), Park (136), and Williamson (164).

(11) See Steinberg and Yager (155), and Wang (161) on other proposals.

(12) (120).

(13) Financial Times, 1st May 1980, 34.

(14) Ortiz-Mena (135), 490-491.

(15) On this point see Guth (69), and Dorrance, (50).

(16) Bird (19).

(17) IMF Survey, 15th October, 1979.

(18) See Bhagwati (ed.): The Brain Drain and Taxation. (North Holland, Amsterdam, 1976).

(19) See especially Harry Johnson's contribution in Bhagwati (ed.) at 361.

(20) Cooper (38), 115.

(21) Cline (35), 344.

(22) Ibid., 340. The principal of "aid graduation" is also supported by Edelman and Chenery (51), and recently, by the World Bank.

(23)   OECD, (133) 234-235.

(24)   Diaz-Alejandro (46) 194.

CHAPTER 11

(1)   The net size of the eurocurrency markets was $945
      billion at the end of March 1982. BIS.

(2)   World Financial Markets December 1979, 6.

(3)   Amex Bank Review. September 1, 1981.

(4)   Reported in The Banker. November, 1981.

(5)   IMF Survey, 19th May, 1980.

(6)   See Einhorn (52).

(7)   IBRD: Co-financing. (Washington D.C., December
      1976).

Bibliography

1. Adler, J.H., (ed.)., 1967, Capital Movements and
    Economic Development. (St. Martin's Press, New
    York).

2. Ahluwalia, M.S., Carter, N.G., and Chenery, H.B.,
    1978, Growth and Poverty in Developing Countries.
    World Bank Staff Working Paper No. 309.

3. Ainley, E.M., 1979, The IMF: Past, Present, and
    Future. Bangor Occasional Papers in Economics,
    No. 15 (University of Wales Press).

4. Aldcroft, D., 1977, From Versailles to Wall Street:
    1919-1929 (Allen Lane, London).

5. Aliber, R.Z., 1977, Living with Developing Country
    Debt, Lloyds Bank Review, October.

6. Bandera, U.N., 1968, Foreign Capital as an Instru-
    ment of National Economic Policy (Martinus Nijhoff,
    The Hague).

7. Barber, A., 1975, Finance for Developing Countries,
    Journal of the Institute of Bankers, August.

8. Bauer, P.T., 1971, Dissent on Development.
    (Weidenfeld and Nicolson, London).

9. Beckerman, W., 1974, In Defence of Economic Growth.
    (Jonathan Cape, London).

10. Bein, D.O., 1978, The Developing Country Debt
    Problem. Development Digest, October.

11. Berrill, K., 1964, Foreign Capital and Take-Off in W.W. Rostow, (ed.), The Economics of Take-Off into sustained growth (Macmillan, London) 285-300.

12. Bhagwati, J., and Desai, P., 1970, India: Planning for Industrialization. (Oxford University Press, London for OECD).

13. Bhagwati, J., et al (eds.), 1971, Trade, Balance of Payments and Growth - Essays in Honour of Charles Kindleberger. (North Holland, Amsterdam).

14. Bhagwati, J., 1971, The Economics of Underdeveloped Countries. (Weidenfeld and Nicolson, London).

15. Bhagwati, J., (ed.), 1978, The New International Economic Order: The North-South Debate, (MIT Press, Massachusetts).

16. Bhagwati, J., 1978, Foreign Trade Regimes and Economic Development: Anatomy and Consequences of Exchange Control Regimes (NBER, New York).

17. Bhagwati, J. and Srinivasan, T., 1979, Trade Policy and Development in R. Dornbusch and J. Frenkel (eds.), International Economic Policy: Theory and Evidence. (John Hopkins Press, Baltimore).

18. Bhatia, R., and Khatkhate, D., 1975, Financial Intermediation, Savings Mobilization, and Entre-preneurial Development: The African Experience, IMF Staff Papers, Vol. 22, 132-158.

19. Bird, G., 1979, An Integrated Programme for Finance and Aid, The Banker, September.

20. Bittermann, H., 1973, The Refunding of International Debt (Duke University Press, North Carolina).

21. Brandt, W., 1980, North-South: A Programme for Sur-vival. Pan Books, London.

22. Brimmer, A., 1971, Central Banking and Economic Development, Journal of Money, Credit and Banking, Vol. 3, No. 4, 780-792.

23. Brittain, W.H., and Cleveland, H., 1978, Are the LDCs over their Heads?, Development Digest, October.

24. Bruton, H.J., 1969, The Two-Gap Approach to Growth
    and Development: Comment, American Economic Review.
    June, 439-446.

25. Burns, A., 1978, Reflections of an Economic
    Policy-maker (American Enterprise Institute,
    Washington).

26. Byres, T.J., (ed.), 1972, Foreign Resources and
    Economic Development (Frank Cass - London).

27. Cairncross, A.K., 1964, Factors in Economic Develop-
    ment (George Allen and Unwin, London).

28. Caldwell, J., and Villamil, J., 1979, U.S. Lenders
    are Learning to Discriminate, Euromoney, April.

29. Cameron, R., (ed.), 1967, Banking in the Early Stages
    of Industrialization (Oxford University Press, New
    York).

30. Cameron, R., (ed.), 1972, Banking and Economic
    Development (Oxford University Press, New York).

31. Chenery, H.B., and Strout, A.M., 1966, Foreign
    Assistance and Economic Development, American Eco-
    nomic Review, Vol. 56, 679-733.

32. Chenery, H.B., 1975, The Structuralist Approach to
    Development, American Economic Review, Vol. 65,
    No. 2, May.

33. Cherniavsky, M., 1978, The World Bank - Paper pre-
    sented to a conference of International Lending
    Agencies in London, and sponsored by the Confedera-
    tion of British Industry, July.

34. Cline, W.R., 1976, International Monetary Reform and
    the Developing Countries (Brookings Institution,
    Washington D.C.).

35. Cline, W.R., (ed.), 1979, Policy Alternatives for a
    New International Economic Order (Praeger, New York).

36. Cole, D.C., 1976, Concepts, Causes, and Cures of
    Instability in LDCs in R. McKinnon (ed.), Money and
    Finance in Economic Growth and Development: Essays
    in Honour of Edward G. Shaw. (Dekker, New York).

37. Committee of London Clearing Banks., 1978, Evidence to the Committee to Review the Functioning of Financial Institutions.

38. Cooper, R.N., and Truman, E.M., 1971, An Analysis of the Role of International Capital Markets in Providing Funds to Developing Countries, Weltwirtschaftliches Archiv, June, 153-183.

39. Cooper, R., 1978, The Oceans as a Source of Revenue, in Bhagwati (ed.), op. cit.

40. Crockett, A., and Knight, M., 1978, International Bank Lending in Perspective, Finance and Development, December.

41. DaCosta, M., and Housty, F., 1977, Foreign Exchange Budgets: Theory and Practice, Paper presented to the Caribbean Monetary Studies Conference, Nassau.

42. Davies, Glyn, 1979, Planning for Economic and Social Development, Mimeo, UWIST, Cardiff.

43. Davis, S.I., 1974, The Euro-Bank: Its Origins, Management, and Outlook, (Macmillan, London).

44. De Roover, R., 1963, The Rise and Decline of the Medici Bank, (Harvard University Press, Cambridge).

45. Devlin, R., 1978, External Finance and Commercial Banks, CEPAL Review, First half.

46. Diaz-Alejandro, C.F., 1976, The post-1971 International Financial System and the Less-developed Countries, in G.K. Helleiner (ed.), A World Divided: The Less-developed countries in the International Economy (Cambridge University Press, Cambridge).

47. Diaz-Alejandro, C.F., 1976, Foreign Trade Regimes and Economic Development: Colombia (NBER, New York).

48. Di Marco, L., (ed.), 1972, International Economics and Development: Essays in Honour of Raul Prebisch (Academic Press, New York).

49. Dizard, J., 1978, The Revolution in Assessing Country Risk, Institutional Investor, October.

50. Dorrance, G., 1981, Would Loan Guarantees Undermine International Capital Markets?, The Banker. December, 39-41.

51. Edelman, J., and Chenery, H.B., 1978, Aid and Income Distribution in Bhagwati, J., (ed.), op. cit.

52. Einhorn, J.P., 1979, Co-operation between Public and Private Lenders to the Third World, The World Economy, Vol. 2, No. 2, May.

53. Einzig, P., 1964, The History of Foreign Exchange (Macmillan, London).

54. Ellis, H.S., (ed.), 1961, Economic Development for Latin America (Macmillan, London).

55. Feder, G., 1978, Economic Growth, Foreign Loans and Debt Servicing Capacity of Developing Countries, World Bank Staff Working Paper, No. 274.

56. Feder, G., and Just, R., 1978, Debt Servicing Capacity and National Policy, Development Digest, October.

57. Fishlow, A., 1978, Debt Remains a Problem, Foreign Policy, Spring.

58. Frank, C.R., and Baird, M., 1976, Foreign Aid: Its Speckled Past and Future Prospects, in C.F. Bergsten and L. Krause (eds.), World Politics and International Economics (Brookings Institution, Washington D.C.).

59. Franko, L.G., 1978, Financing Economic Development, Journal of World Trade Law, Vol. 12, No. 2.

60. Friedman, I.S., 1977, The Emerging Role of Private Banks in the Developing World (Citicorp, New York).

61. Friedman, I.S., 1978, Country Risk: The Lessons of Zaire, The Banker, February.

62. Galbis, V., 1977, Financial Intermediation and Economic Growth in Less-developed Countries: A Theoretical Approach, in P.C. Ayre (ed.), Finance in Developing Countries (Frank Cass, London).

63. Gerschenkron, A., 1966, Economic Backwardness in Historical Perspective (Harvard University Press, Cambridge).

64. Goldsmith, R.W., 1969, Financial Structure and Development (Yale University Press, New Haven).

65. Grayson, L.E., 1973, The Role of Suppliers' Credits in the Industrialization of Ghana, Economic Development and Cultural Change, Vol. 21, 477-499.

66. Green, R., 1976, Aspects of the World Monetary and Resource Transfer System: A View from the Extreme Periphery, in G. Helleiner (ed.), op. cit.

67. Grubel, H., (ed.), 1963, World Monetary Reform (Stanford University Press, Stanford).

68. Gurley, J., and Shaw, E.S., 1955, Financial Aspects of Economic Development, American Economic Review, Vol. 45, September.

69. Guth, W., 1979, Sources of Finance for Development, Journal of the Institute of Bankers, Vol. 100, October.

70. Haan, R.L., 1971, Special Drawing Rights and Development (Stenfert Kroese, The Netherlands).

71. Hagen, E., 1968, The Economics of Development (Irwin, New York).

72. Hahn, R.F., and Matthews, R.C.O., 1964, The Theory of Economic Growth: A Survey, The Economic Journal, Vol. 74, December.

73. Halm, G.N., 1975, A Guide to International Monetary Reform (Lexington Books, D.C. Heath and Co., Massachusetts).

74. Hang-Shen Cheng, 1977, Commercial Bank Financing of World Payment Imbalances, Federal Reserve Bank of San Francisco Economic Review, Fall.

75. Hewson, J. and Sakakibara, E., 1975, The Eurocurrency Markets and Their Implications (Lexington Books, D.C. Heath and Co. Massachusetts).

76. Hirschman, A.O., and Bird, R.M., 1968, Foreign Aid: A Critique and a Proposal, Princeton Essays in International Finance, No. 69.

77. Horvat, B., 1967, Comment on Prof. Kafka's paper: Economic Effects of Capital Imports, in Adler (ed.), op. cit.

78. Hughes, H., 1979, Debt and Development: The Role of Foreign Capital in Economic Growth, World Development, 95-112.

79. Islam, N., 1976, The External Debt Problem of the Developing Countries with Special Reference to the Least-developed, in Helleiner (ed.), op. cit.

80. Johnson, H.G., 1967, Economic Policies Toward Less-developed Countries (George Allen and Unwin, London).

81. Johnson, H.G., 1968, Money, Trade, and Economic Growth (George Allen and Unwin, London).

82. Johnson, H.G., 1968, International Monetary Reform and the Less-developed countries in his, Essays in Monetary Economics, (George Allen and Unwin, London).

83. Johnson, H.G., 1972, The Ideology of Economic Policy in the New States, in D. Wall (ed.), Chicago Essays in Economic Development (University of Chicago Press, Chicago).

84. Johnson, H.G., 1976, Towards a World Central Bank, The Banker, February.

85. Jones, H., 1975, An Introduction to Modern Theories of Economic Growth (Nelson, London).

86. Joshi, V., 1979, Exchange Rates, International Liquidity and Economic Development, The World Economy, Vol. 2, No. 2, May.

87. Kapur, I., 1977, The Supply of Eurocurrency Finance to Developing Countries, Finance and Development, September.

88. Kelly, A.C., Williamson, J., and Cheetham, R.,
    1972, Dualistic Economic Development: Theory and
    History (University of Chicago Press, Chicago).

89. Kindleberger, C.P., 1970, Less-developed Countries
    and the International Capital Market, in J. Markham
    and G. Papanek (eds.), Industrial Organization and
    Economic Development in Honour of E.S. Mason
    (Houghton Mifflin Co., New York).

90. Kindleberger, C.P., 1972, The Benefits of Interna-
    tional Money, Journal of International Economics,
    Vol. 2, 425-442.

91. Kindleberger, C.P., 1976, International Financial
    Intermediation for Developing Countries, in
    R. McKinnon (ed.), op. cit.

92. Kirshner, J., (ed.), 1974, Business, Banking and
    Economic Thought in Late Medieval and Early Modern
    Europe (University of Chicago Press, Chicago).

93. Krassowski, A., 1974, Development and the Debt Trap:
    Economic Planning and External Borrowing in Ghana
    (Croom Helm, London).

94. Krueger, A., 1978, Foreign Trade Regimes and Eco-
    nomic Development: Liberalization Attempts and
    Consequences (NBER, New York).

95. Leeson, P.F., 1979, The Lewis Model and Development
    Theory, The Manchester School, September, 196-210.

96. Leff, N., 1975, Rates of Return to Capital, Domestic
    Savings, and Investment in the Developing
    Countries, Kyklos, Vol. 28, No. 4.

97. Leith, J.C., 1974, Foreign Trade Regimes and Eco-
    nomic Development: Ghana, (NBER, New York).

98. Lewis, A.W., 1954, Economic Development with
    Unlimited Supplies of Labour, The Manchester
    School, May, 131-191.

99. Lewis, A.W., 1972, The Theory of Economic Growth
    (George Allen and Unwin, London).

100. Lewis, A.W., 1977, The LDCs and Stable Exchange Rates, 1977 Per Jacobsson Lecture (IMF, Washington D.C.).

101. Lewis, A.W., 1978, Growth and Fluctuations: 1870-1913 (George Allen and Unwin, London).

102. Lewis, A.W., 1978, The Evolution of the International Economic Order (Princeton University Press, Princeton).

103. Lewis, A.W., 1979, Prospects for World Development, in The Financing of Long-Term Development, Papers presented to the 32nd International Banking Summer School, held at St. John's College, Cambridge, August. (The Institute of Bankers, London).

104. Lewis, A.W., 1979, The Dual Economy Re-visited, The Manchester School, September, 211-229.

105. Lipton, M., 1977, Why Poor People Stay Poor: A Study of Urban Bias in World Development (Temple Smith, London).

106. Little, I., Scitovsky, T., and Scott, M., 1970, Industry and Trade in Some Developing Countries (Oxford University Press, London).

107. Llewellyn, D.T., 1979, International Financial Intermediation in S. Frowen (ed.), A Framework of International Banking (Guildford Educational Press, Surrey).

108. Macbean, R.I., and Balasubramanyam, V.N., 1978, Meeting the Third World Challenge (Macmillan, London).

109. Machlup, F., 1972, Introduction in F. Machlup, W W. Salant, and L. Tarshis (eds.), International Mobility and Movement of Capital (NBER, New York).

110. Maizels, S., 1976, A New International Strategy for Primary Commodities, in G.K. Helleiner (ed.), op. cit.

111. Mckenzie, C.W., 1976, The Economics of the Euro-currency System (Macmillan, London).

112. Mckinnon, R.I., 1964, Foreign Exchange Constraints in Economic Development and Efficient Aid Allocation, Economic Journal, Vol, 74, 388-409.
113. Mckinnon, R.I., 1973, Money and Capital in Economic Development (Brookings Institution, Washington D.C.).
114. Mckinnon, R.I., 1974, Money, Growth, and the Propensity to Save: An Iconoclastic View, in G. Horwich and P. Samuelson (eds.), Trade, Stability and Macroeconomics: Essays in Honour of Lloyd A. Metzler (Academic Press, New York).
115. Mckinnon, R.I., 1979, Money in International Exchange (Oxford University Press, New York).
116. Mcnamara, R., 1979, The High Cost of Protectionism, Institutional Investor, September.
117. Meier, G.M., (ed.), 1970, Leading Issues in Economic Development (Oxford University Press, New York).
118. Meier, G.M., 1976, Implications of International Monetary Reform for Less-developed Countries, in Y. Aharoni (ed.), The Emerging International Monetary Order and the Banking System (University Publishing Projects, Tel Aviv).
119. Michalopoulos, C., 1968, Imports, Foreign Exchange, and Economic Development: The Greek Experience, in P.B. Kenen and R. Lawrence (eds.), The Open Economy (Columbia University Press, New York).
120. Michalopoulos, C., Financing Needs of Developing Countries: Proposals for International Actions, in, The International Monetary System and the Developing Nations (Agency for International Development, Washington D.C.).
121. Mikesell, R.F., 1968, The Economics of Foreign Aid (Weidenfeld and Nicolson, London).

122. Miki, T., and Okita, S., 1967, Treatment of Foreign
     Capital - A Case Study for Japan, in J. Adler (ed.),
     op. cit.

123. Morgan, E.V., and Thomas, W., 1962, The Stock
     Exchange: Its History and Functions (Elek Books,
     London).

124. Morse, J., 1979, The International Monetary System
     and the Financing of Long-term Development,
     Journal of the Institute of Bankers, Vol. 100,
     No. 4, August.

125. Moskowitz, W.E., 1979, Global Asset and Liability
     Management of Commercial Banks, Federal Reserve
     Bank of New York Quarterly Review, Spring.

126. Myint, H., 1971, Economic Theory and the Under-
     developed Countries (Oxford University Press, New
     York).

127. Myint, H., 1973, The Economics of Developing
     Countries (Hutchinson, London).

128. Myrdal, G., 1959, An International Economy
     (Routledge and Keegan Paul, London).

129. Nafziger, E.W., 1979, A Critique of Development
     Economics in the U.S., in D. Lehmann (ed.),
     Development Theory - Four Critical Studies
     (Frank Cass, London).

130. Nagy, P., 1978, Country Risk: How to Assess,
     Quantify and Monitor It (Euromoney Publications,
     London).

131. Nagy, P., 1979, It's Time to Call in the Commercial
     Banks, Euromoney, February.

132. OECD., 1979, The Impact of the Newly-Industrializing
     Countries on Production and Trade in Manufactures
     (OECD, Paris).

133. OECD., 1981, Development Co-operation, 1981 Review
     (OECD, Paris).

134. Ohlin, G., 1976, Debts, Development and Default, in
      G.K. Helleiner (ed.), op. cit.

135. Ortiz-Mena, A., 1975, Development in Latin America
      - A View from the IDB (IDB, Washington D.C.).

136. Park, Y.S., 1973, The Link Between SDRs and
      Development Finance, Princeton Essays in Interna-
      tional Finance, No. 100.

137. Patrick, H.T., 1966, Financial Development and Eco-
      nomic Growth in Underdeveloped Countries, Economic
      Development and Cultural Change, Vol. 14, 174-189.

138. Pazos, F., 1961, Private versus Public Foreign
      Investment in Underdeveloped Areas, in H.S. Ellis
      (ed.), op. cit.

139. Perera, P., 1968, Development Finance: Institutions,
      Problems, and Prospects (Praeger, New York).

140. Please, S., 1971, Mobilizing Internal Resources
      Through Taxation, in R. Robinson (ed.), Developing
      the Third World (Cambridge University Press,
      London).

141. Resnick, S.A., 1975, State of Development Economics,
      American Economic Review, Vol. 65, No. 2, May.

142. Reynolds, L.G., 1970, Is 'Development Economics' a
      Subject?, in J.W. Markham and G. Papanek (eds.),
      op. cit.

143. Richman, B., 1975, Chinese and Indian Development:
      An Interdisciplinary Environmental Analysis,
      American Economic Review, Vol. 65, No. 2, May.

144. Rockefeller, D., 1973, The Future Environment of
      World-Wide Banking, 3rd Jane Hodge Memorial
      Lecture, UWIST, Cardiff.

145. Rockefeller, D., 1974, Financial Aspects of the
      Energy Situation, Speech delivered at the 1974
      International Monetary Conference, Williamsburg,
      Virginia, June.

158

146. Ruding, H.O., 1978, The IMF and International
      Credit, The Banker, June.
147. Salant, W., 1972, Financial Intermediation As An
      Explanation of Enduring Deficits in the Balance of
      Payments, in F. Machlup et al (eds.), op. cit.
148. Sargen, N., 1976, Commercial Bank Lending to
      Developing Countries, Federal Reserve Bank of San
      Francisco Economic Review, Spring.
149. Sargen, N., 1977, Economic Indicators and Country
      Risk Appraisal, Federal Reserve Bank of San
      Francisco Economic Review, Fall.
150. Sayers, R.S., 1957, Lloyds Bank in the History of
      English Banking (Oxford University Press, London).
151. Schumpeter, J., 1964, Business Cycles (McGraw Hill,
      New York). (First published in 1939).
152. Sen, A.K., (ed.), 1970, Growth Economics (Penguin,
      London).
153. Shaw, E.S., 1973, Financial Deepening in Economic
      Development (Oxford University Press, New York).
154. Spellman, L.J., 1976, Economic Growth and Financial
      Intermediation, in R.I. McKinnon (ed.), op. cit.
155. Steinberg, E.B., and Yager, J., 1978, New Means of
      Financing International Needs (Brookings Institu-
      tion, Washington D.C.).
156. Streeten, P., 1977, The Frontiers of Development
      Studies (Macmillan, London).
157. Streeten, P., and Burki, S., 1978, Basic Needs:
      Some Issues, World Development, Vol. 6, No. 3,
      411-421.
158. Tendler, J., 1975, Inside Foreign Aid (John Hopkins
      University Press, Maryland).
159. Thomas, B., 1967, The Historical Record of Interna-
      tional Capital Movements to 1913, in J. Adler
      (ed.), op. cit.

160. Ul Haq, M., 1967, Tied Credits: A Quantitative Analysis, in J. Adler (ed.), op. cit.

161. Wang, N.T., 1977, New Proposals for the International Finance of Development, Princeton Essays in International Finance, No. 59.

162. Weisskopf, T.E., 1972, Capitalism, Underdevelopment and the Future of the Poor Countries, in J. Bhagwati (ed.), Economics and World Order - From the 1970s to the 1990s (Macmillan, New York) 43-77.

163. Wellons, P., 1977, Borrowing by Developing Countries on the Eurocurrency Market (OECD, Paris).

164. Williamson, J., 1978, SDRs: The Link, in J. Bhagwati (ed.), op. cit.

165. Witteveen, J., 1978, Financing the LDCs: The Role of Public and Private Institutions, Speech delivered at the 1978 Euromarkets Conference held in London, May.

166. World Bank, World Development Reports 1979-1981 (Oxford University Press, London).

167. Yamamura, K., 1972, Japan - 1868-1930: A Revised View, in R. Cameron (ed.), op. cit.

168. Yungchul Park, 1973, The Role of Money in Stabilization Policy in Developing Countries, IMF Staff Papers, Vol. 20.

Index